The Art of Bitfulness

the art of bitfulness

KEEPING CALM IN THE DIGITAL WORLD

NANDAN NILEKANI

TANUJ BHOJWANI

PENGUIN
ALLEN
LANE

An imprint of Penguin Random House

ALLEN LANE

USA | Canada | UK | Ireland | Australia
New Zealand | India | South Africa | China

Allen Lane is part of the Penguin Random House group of companies
whose addresses can be found at global.penguinrandomhouse.com

Published by Penguin Random House India Pvt. Ltd
4th Floor, Capital Tower 1, MG Road,
Gurugram 122 002, Haryana, India

First published in Allen Lane by Penguin Random House India 2022

ISBN 9780670094790

For sale in the Indian Subcontinent only

Typeset in Sabon by Manipal Technologies Limited, Manipal
Printed at Replika Press Pvt. Ltd, India

www.penguin.co.in

To Tanush, Janhavi, Shray, Nihar and Rohini
—Nandan Nilekani

*To my parents, Lalit and Radhika, who taught me how to be
curious; and therefore everything else.*
—Tanuj Bhojwani

CONTENTS

PART ONE

THE PROBLEM

1

A TOXIC RELATIONSHIP

OUR TOOLS

About eight hours before his flight, Prabhkiran Singh got a text from his friend that he was backing out of their vacation.

As the CEO of a growing start-up, Bewakoof, Prabhkiran often felt like he could never switch off from work. He had made plans with a friend to take a week-long vacation to Port Blair. He had booked flight tickets but had not done much else to plan the vacation. Prabhkiran decided he still needed the break, so he set an alarm and texted his friend to say he was still going to go.

Port Blair is the capital city of Andaman and Nicobar Islands, located in the Bay of Bengal, about 1400 kilometres away from the Indian mainland. In August 2020, the Indian government finished laying an optical fibre between the islands and the mainland. This optical fibre finally enabled 4G services and wired broadband on the islands. What this means is that if you landed there in 2017, as Prabhkiran had, you'd switch on your phone to find that you didn't have any cellular data or Wi-Fi and, consequently, no access to the internet.

Landing in a new place without the internet was strange and made Prabhkiran slightly nervous. He couldn't look up hotels or make reservations online. He couldn't look up a map to decide where to go or book a taxi to go there. He hadn't even saved any music on his phone because he was used to the idea of streaming music on demand. Prabhkiran admits that when he first realized there was no internet, he slightly regretted his decision to fly unprepared. But, over the next seven days, he had the best vacation he has ever had.

Instead of looking things up on his phone, Prabhkiran had to talk to people to make his way around. When bored, he couldn't scroll social media or sneak a peek at his email. Once he reached the resort, not only was there no internet, there was no cellular reception either. Most days, he didn't even carry his phone with him. The best part was that everyone else on the island was disconnected too. He found that people were more sociable and friendly. Strangers would join him for dinner and share stories from their travels. Prabhkiran carried a book every time he'd go on vacation, but this was the first time he actually finished reading it. After a very long time, he felt present in the moment and at peace.

By the end of his vacation to the islands, Prabhkiran realized that being unplugged wasn't as scary as he had first imagined. He vowed to spend less time on his phone and more time amidst nature or in the company of friends. He deleted social media apps from his phone. After his return to Mumbai, every day, at 5.30 p.m. sharp, he would leave his phone on his desk and walk with a friend to Powai Lake to soak in the sunset. He found himself less stressed and more in control of his day.

If this were a movie, this is where the story would have ended.

You probably know what happened next. For a few weeks, Prabhkiran still caught the sunset every day, but he started taking his phone with him. Eventually, he stopped going. First one, then another; soon, all the social media apps came back. Work slowly started eating into his personal life, and Prabhkiran found himself exactly where he began—feeling overworked, overwhelmed and always connected.

We all know this conflict. Our devices make our lives incredibly convenient, but at the same time, they take something away from the quality of our lives. Yet, it is impractical to disconnect. Prabhkiran, for instance, would be unable to run his company without his smartphone. Even cutting down screen time is very hard. We may be able to do it for a few days or weeks, but, eventually, we all slip up and get back to where we started.

In an ideal world, our technology would be less distracting, and we'd be less easily distracted. We, however, do not live in an ideal world. Our technology is addictive by design, and we're easily addicted by nature. Focusing on only one side of this problematic equation will tell an incomplete story. This book is an attempt at fixing the relationship we have with our digital tools, by looking at both sides of the equation.

We must begin by understanding how we shaped our tools and how they, in turn, are shaping us.

OUR EXTENDED MINDS

Most tools and technologies we've invented for a major part of human existence involved manipulating atoms and energy, amplifying the work our bodies could do. The steam engine, the fundamental invention of the industrial revolution, allowed us to convert heat into mechanical work. The information revolution had a different aim. Computers could manipulate bits of information, amplifying what our brains could do.

Over forty years ago, in 1980, Steve Jobs called the personal computer the 'bicycle of the mind'. Compared with the technology of 1980, today we have the equivalent of personal Formula 1 race cars and 16-lane 'broadband' highways to connect the whole world. There has been a ridiculous increase in the capacity, capability and velocity of information technologies. They remain, however, a vehicle for our minds to augment how we think and sense. In their purpose, therefore, not much has changed.

Instead of viewing information technology as something outside of ourselves, we want to look at all aspects related to information technology—our computers, smartphones, smart devices, the apps on them and the data we access through them—as being prosthetics for our brain. Every time we use these technologies—searching for something online, clicking a like button, paying on an e-commerce site, sending a text to a friend or taking any other action—we generate a data trail. This data trail is the electronic manifestation of a thought that originated in our minds. Our data fuels these information technologies, but it is not any new oil—it is our *naked selves*.

Our devices, all the software that runs them and the data that powers them, are an extension of our mind.

Our extended minds support the way we think, talk and engage with the world. In the obvious sense, we connect with our friends over social media, instant messages or phone calls. In the less obvious sense, what we talk about offline is shaped by what we see online. Even in offline, face-to-face interactions, we pull out our phones to share pictures, videos or texts. Our extended minds help us share what we see and experience, enriching our connection with others.

Even if we don't call technology an extension of the mind, we can still feel it. Most of us would hesitate to hand over our unlocked smartphones to others. The loss of privacy online makes us feel violated in real life. Simply running out of charge on their smartphones gives most people anxiety. If you've lost a phone or a hard disk with personal data you hadn't backed up, you know what you felt is genuine grief.

Over the last two decades, digital technologies have integrated into all parts of our lives. Our extended minds are now an essential part of how we live, love, learn, and earn. There is a good reason for the growing influence of digital technology in our lives—they can often feel like superpowers.

Do you remember the first time you booked a taxi using a ride-sharing app? For those of us old enough to remember the uncertainty of finding a taxi on the streets, apps like Meru, Uber or Ola were nothing less than magic. There's every reason to believe the future will have more inventions that make our lives better. Therefore, we are not advocating ways to disconnect or detox, only to go back to the same problems in a few weeks as Prabhkiran did.

We don't want to avoid these superpowers. We want to avoid the kryptonite that comes along with them. This book does not look at technology as something outside of ourselves that we need to minimize. Instead, we want to integrate technology into our lives to help us achieve what we want. The idea behind this book is not to spend less time on our devices.

The goal is to spend our time on our devices *better*.

OUR RELATIONSHIP WITH OUR TECHNOLOGY

In the conversations that led to this book, the most common complaint we heard was losing a sense of time.

Dhruv described it best with his experience. Dhruv is a musician. As much as he loves his job, there are tasks he doesn't like doing. One such task is doing receipts and balancing the accounts for the studio and equipment rental. It was 3.55 p.m., so he decided to browse Instagram for five minutes before cracking on with the task.

It was 5.07 p.m. when Dhruv finally realized he had ended up going down a rabbit hole. He felt a sudden pang of guilt and shut the Instagram app. He was in a state of panic because he had lost time. His mind started to race, thinking about the task ahead. Almost involuntarily, Dhruv did what he often does when he's feeling anxious—surf Instagram. It was nearly 5.30 p.m. before he realized he'd done it again.

Dhruv explains, 'I find myself browsing social media automatically. After twenty minutes, I won't even remember what I was looking at, and whatever I just saw would mean nothing to me. Somehow I keep going back for more.'

Instagram is relatively new; the problem Dhruv describes is not. People have been procrastinating since millennia. Our specific form of distraction may be new, but the part of the equation that has remained constant is us and our tendency to avoid certain tasks. We all care about making our lives better, so why do we not do what we definitely know will help us?

After decades of research, scientists now believe that procrastination is not a time-management problem but an emotion-management problem. We feel good when we finish the task at hand. But we also know that the act of doing the task will not make us feel great. It could be tedious, stressful, or maybe we are just afraid of not doing it well. Whatever be the particular reason for our anxiety about the task, our brain procrastinates to prevent us from facing those anxieties.

When we take the human propensity for procrastination and add a smartphone to it, we have a recipe for disaster.

Our smartphones encourage a behaviour where we instantly act on our every fleeting whim. We pick up our phones and start searching or scrolling on autopilot. The starting point may be finding an answer to an innocent question, recollecting the name of a song we'd heard weeks ago, or simply wondering what our friends are up to. Each new result leads to another question, and another search. We promise ourselves to get back to what we were doing after this one quick digression. The answer we seek always remains a click away.

Dhruv's experience is not unique, nor is it specific to Instagram. Everyone we spoke to has experienced this lost sense of time. It is not always social media either. Sometimes it's the news, games or simply going through Wikipedia, page after page. There's nothing inherently wrong with five minutes of Instagram or YouTube or whichever app catches our fancy. The problem is that it hardly ever stays just five minutes. Instead of looking at each app as an attention problem or a privacy problem, let's step back and ask a larger question:

What is the nature of our relationship with our technology?

We've become co-dependent on these technologies. They need us to give them attention, and we need them to take our attention away from our problems. Yes, these technologies are addictive, but we're not just addicted to 'tweets' or 'stories'. We're addicted to avoiding our anxieties and boredom, and our smartphones are more than happy to oblige us with an infinite feed of distractions.

We want our technology to be a trusted sidekick, make our jobs more manageable, and support the life we want. We want it to free up our time so that we can accomplish more. Often it becomes that toxic friend—one who indulges our vices, makes our jobs harder, and demands more than we can give. It often takes up so much of our time that we end up feeling like we aren't doing enough with our lives.

Most of us are in a toxic relationship with our technology and in denial about it. It is why taking a break can feel liberating, as Prabhkiran felt in Port Blair. It is also why once we get back to our daily lives, we repeat the patterns of co-dependency, only to get right back to where we started.

The only way to fix this relationship is to take an honest look at how we use our extended mind. We need to fix the *patterns* that cause us to lose our time, attention and privacy.

INTRODUCING THE ART OF BITFULNESS

Even without the distractions of modern technology, our attention wavers often.

Science tells us that our mind wanders for about 50 per cent of our waking hours, making it hard for us to keep our attention on the task at hand. Add poor mood, stress or threat of danger (like a global pandemic due to a novel virus), and this number goes up. In March–April of 2020, just as most nations in the Western world started entering lockdowns, the number of people searching for 'meditation' went up by as much as 100 per cent.

Amishi Jha is the associate professor of psychology and director of contemplative neuroscience, Mindfulness Research & Practice Initiative at the University of Miami. Her research focuses on the brain bases of attention, working memory, and mindfulness-based training. She studies what causes attention to wander and, most importantly, how to bring it back.

Jha describes attention as a flashlight. There's far too much information in our environments for our brain to meaningfully absorb. When we move the flashlight of our attention on one thing, it allows us to ignore information from everything else. If our brains are computers, our attention is the processor's control unit. As Jha writes, 'Wherever attention goes, the rest of the brain follows—in some sense, attention is your brain's boss. But is it a good boss, and can we train it?'

According to Jha and her more than eighteen years of research, the simple answer is—yes. You can train your attention with practice. The way to do it is to practise mindfulness. Jha explains, 'From our work, we're learning that the opposite of a stressed and wandering mind is a mindful one. Mindfulness has to do with paying attention to our present moment experience with awareness and without any kind of emotional reactivity of what's happening.'

The critical idea in mindfulness is not to look at a wandering mind as something inherently good or inherently bad. It is something that simply is. What matters is our persistent but gentle effort to bring our minds back to the present moment. A good metaphor is to imagine oneself sitting on a bench at a busy railway station. The trains that pass through are our thoughts. Typically, our mind tends to follow these thoughts causing us anxiety or stress. We may try to block or stop the thoughts, which only backfires. The key idea is to notice the trains come and go without reacting emotionally.

Over time, bringing our attention back to the present becomes a skill. We start seeing the benefits of the ability to be present on our entire life. We realize that sometimes our impulsive first thought does not need to be chased down. People who practise mindfulness report being better able to handle stress, modulate emotional responses and deal with distractions.

One way to frame our toxic relationship with technology is that our extended mind is wandering. Instead of helping our brains think, these technologies amplify the tendency of our minds to wander. Our devices have given us the ability to chase every train of thought, and it is hard to keep it focused on the right one. Practising mindfulness helps focus our minds on the present, ignoring stray thoughts. Can we learn how to focus our extended minds too?

Our struggle with our technology is part of a challenging class of problems. We struggle to keep our weight in control in an age of readily available high-sugar and high-fat foods. We know that obesity is associated with many diseases. Yet, this knowledge is insufficient to cover the gap in practice. We experience the same problem when trying to quit addictive substances such as cigarettes and alcohol.

The most common misconception whether we're trying to lose weight, quit smoking or focus our extended mind is that it requires an iron will. In fact, for success, we need precisely the opposite. There are numerous behaviour change studies which demonstrate that instead of relying on maintaining willpower, we are more likely to succeed if we change our environment to avoid junk food or cigarettes. Instead of aiming to lose ten kilograms, you want to focus on something in your immediate control, like not snacking between meals. You want to make small changes, each adding up bit by bit, to create healthier habits that are easy to maintain, even on days when your willpower is low. The desired outcomes automatically follow.

While we can't change our minds to start disliking high-sugar or high-fat foods, the good news is that our extended minds are programmable. We can spend some time becoming aware of how we falter and then put systems in place to prevent it from happening. Instead of exerting willpower to stay focused, we can design our technology to guide our attention to the task at hand. We can sustain new digital habits much more effortlessly than dieting or exercising because we can configure our devices to assist us instead of distracting us.

This awareness-driven environment design and habit change are what we call *The Art of Bitfulness*.

We, the authors, have both personally experienced frustration from technology overwhelming us. We have also found that it exists, to varying extents, amongst our friends and colleagues. Everyone we know has come up with their own rules and strategies to manage the overwhelm. Nandan, for example, does not use any instant messaging apps—he sends and receives SMSes only. For Tanuj, most of his contacts are on WhatsApp. But the way we deal with messages is similar. Using them as and when required rather than letting incoming notifications dictate our attention. Those few friends, family and colleagues who may need to reach us urgently know which channels to use and our devices are configured to let them. Some differences in our approach emerge due to the age at which we started using these technologies. Nandan got a smartphone only at age fifty-five. Tanuj had one since he was twenty-one. Being in very different stages of life, we had different aims for our extended minds. Being connected to friends was essential to Tanuj, and he made allowances for limited use of social media. Nandan believes social media is not very useful for him. So, he sends emails to his friends or picks up the phone to call them if he can.

Despite the thirty-four-year age difference between us, we found that we have a lot in common in our approaches to manage our relationship with technology. We realized that there were principles that remained common, even though the specific apps or technologies we used to attain similar goals varied. We both also acknowledge that giving up the internet is not a desired option for us. This book, therefore, does not recommend quitting or detoxing from any particular technology. The aim is to have a sense of calm and control over our interaction with our technology.

We both believe taking a thoughtful approach towards when, where and how we interact with our technology has greatly benefited our sense of well-being. So how do we go about fixing our toxic relationship with technology and being more *bitful*?

As with all toxic relationships, you don't focus on the people; you focus on the patterns.

2

THE PROBLEM WITH US

THE HARDEST THING

A December 2020 survey of 2000 Indian urban smartphone users revealed that, on average, users spent 6.9 hours on their smartphones every day. About 74 per cent said they get moody and irritable when they stop using their mobile phones. While 73 per cent said they 'feel compelled' to check their smartphones continually.

'84 per cent people check their phones within the first 15 minutes of waking up, and 46 per cent respondents said they pick up the phone at least five times in an hour-long conversation meeting with friends', said the India Director for the smartphone brand that had commissioned the report.

In the same report, 70 per cent agreed that if their usage continues at the current rate or grows, it is likely to impact their mental or physical health. Seventy-four per cent of respondents agreed that it's vital for them to have a life separate from their mobile phones, and 73 per cent agreed that they would be happier if they spent less time on their smartphones.

By definition, it takes two to make a toxic relationship.

A lot has been said about social media companies and their role in users feeling the compulsive need to check their phones. As any therapist will tell you, fixing a toxic relationship requires genuine self-reflection. It means acknowledging that it is not just your partner to blame. Your own responses and behaviours also contribute to the unhealthy pattern of behaviour. In this chapter, we want to pause and reflect on our role in this situation.

The data is stark. Most users seem to understand that spending excessive time on their phones is a severe problem affecting their well-being. Yet, we continue to use our phones compulsively. What makes us repeat these behaviour patterns that we know are not helpful?

Exercising any sort of self-control is known to be 'phenomenologically aversive'. In plain English, doing what we know we should do *feels* hard. The science behind why we do not act in our own self-interest still puzzles scientists, but the effect is well-documented. Your own experience probably corroborates these findings. Whether it is losing weight or quitting smoking cigarettes, you probably know how *exhausting* it feels to keep going, even when you know what's right for you.

Exercising self-control in our relationship with technology is even more challenging. Every time we use our phones or computers, we make a lot of tiny decisions. Should you check your email now that you have unlocked your phone? Should you reply to that instant message or do it later? Our devices give us the capacity to follow every stray thought or worry at any time. Every moment with our devices tests our self-control. Is it any surprise then that we often falter?

In this chapter, we go over the three ways in which our devices demand our self-control. These three demands on our self-control combine and wear down our ability to make good decisions. Sooner or later, we all get tired and decide to give in. We enter a state of mindless scrolling or bingeing that we later regret.

If we want to spend our time on our devices better, we first need to understand what makes it so hard.

#1 SWITCHING CONTEXTS IS HARD

The big problem with content feeds on the internet is that they are infinite. Even before the internet, the volume of books, periodicals, radio and TV shows available was far greater than our capacity to consume them. So why does this glut of information bother us so much more now?

Before the internet, there were barriers to how we could consume that information. We had to go to a library, or purchase a magazine, or settle down in front of the television at a fixed time to consume content. Our environment gave us clues that helped us put boundaries around tasks and stay in context.

We can now look up almost any book, magazine, movie or television show instantly and anywhere, on demand with nearly zero physical effort. Our computers and our smartphones function as our TV, typewriter, library, calculator, newspaper, video game console, gossip line, among many other things. Worst of all, it is all of these things all of the time. It is not just the amount of information but also our *access* to information that has increased dramatically.

In theory, having access to all this information should help us live better. In practice, it quickly becomes a trap. When we have access to all the information in the world, we don't have to spend time or energy memorizing. Instead, we have a new problem.

Every moment, we need to decide what to focus on.

Before we had always-available access to the internet, our options were limited to what was available in our physical environment and context. Digital technologies allow us to access any context from any environment. With the internet's infinite choice, the responsibility of being disciplined and exerting self-control falls on us.

If you worked in an open-office environment, you'd be less likely to open social media or a game on your desktop during work hours. You'd be worried that your colleagues would see what you're up to. But your smartphone is small and private. You may have turned on your phone for a legitimate purpose but ended up checking distracting content. From the outside, no one can tell what you're up to.

Digital technologies dissolve boundaries and muddle contexts that are sharply defined in equivalent analogue technologies. We switch rapidly and often between work and leisure, not fully immersed in either. You feel like you don't get enough done at work and bring it home. At home, you feel like you're not paying enough attention to your loved ones because you're also engaged in work. If the pandemic made you work remotely from home, this boundary probably became increasingly blurry. Even though you are in one environment, your mind can be in another. Our phones, due to their sizes and designs, are most guilty of promoting this frequent context switching.

Context switching happens on our computers too. As most applications moved to the internet, much of our time and attention on our computers shifted to the browser. Too many open tabs slow down one's computer. They also act as a reminder of the tasks we need to get done, adding to our stress. Since our work, entertainment, and social life are all just tabs, it's tough to stay focused.

Smartphones and browsers let us follow our stray thoughts into virtual worlds. Especially our phones—which allow us to dwell on every little worry that crosses our mind at any time. It could be during dinner with family, when some stray remark about money made us start thinking about how our investments are performing, and we end up interrupting family time to check on our investments, just because we can.

Recently, many people have started measuring the time we spend on the screen. It is pertinent to note that total screen time hides the fact that we're not focused on the task at hand for a few minutes before and after each distraction. We're constantly switching contexts due to these interruptions. Switching contexts has cognitive costs. It is hard to get back to the task we were doing before the interruption.

Screen time doesn't tell the whole story

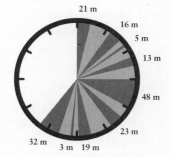

3 HOURS OF SCREEN TIME...

... TRANSLATES TO 7 HOURS OF DISTRACTED EFFORT

The way you use your screen is as important as how long you use it

Researchers have found that most humans are terrible at multitasking. Yet, we overestimate our ability to multitask. We can multitask when using different physical faculties, such as walking and listening to a podcast. But when we have to do two things that require the same attentional circuits, such as writing a document and replying to texts simultaneously, we suffer on both tasks. It takes time to switch contexts, and our focus doesn't bounce back as quickly. Overall, we feel more stressed and get less done.

Computers are general-purpose machines, i.e., unlike a screwdriver which can only perform one function, people use computers for many different purposes. Computers work significantly faster than humans and can do these many things simultaneously. Multitasking is their strength, but our weakness. Humans are good at doing only one thing at a time. Yet, our digital lives are designed around the computers' multitasking ability rather than humans' single-tasking nature.

Every moment you spend on your devices, you must exert self-control to maintain boundaries and preserve context. By design, it is incredibly easy to falter.

#2 CHOOSING IS HARD

In 2000, psychologists Sheena Iyengar and Mark Lepper published a study on the 'paradox of choice'. They presented one set of shoppers at a supermarket with an assortment of twenty-four gourmet jams. To another set of shoppers, they displayed an assortment of only six jams. In their experiment, the larger assortment drew more visitors. But those shoppers were only 1/10th as likely to purchase something compared to those shown only six jams. Though the smaller assortment pulled less of a crowd, its shoppers chose meaningfully and purchased what they liked.

This anomaly in our behaviour came to be known as the 'paradox of choice'. Further studies have shown that excess choice not only produces a 'choice paralysis', but even for those who do choose, it reduces satisfaction with their choices. Choice paralysis holds when choosing between chocolates, paintings and even jobs. Too many options lead to many 'what-if?'s. Even with the freedom to choose exactly what we want, we end up being more unhappy with what we've chosen.

We already see this happening in the online sphere. Many users complain of indecision due to the many choices of what to watch on Netflix or YouTube. Or worse, of spending thirty minutes on deciding what to order from Swiggy or Zomato. We browse through catalogues, hoping to find something that will surprise or delight us. The endless choice encourages a behaviour where the act of deciding itself becomes addictive, keeping us hooked to the product. We hear a similar complaint about dating apps. The easy, instant reward of a new match over the challenging, time-consuming task of building an authentic connection keeps people addicted to swiping. We end up dissatisfied because we spend more time deciding what we'd like than liking what we've decided.

THE PARADOX OF CHOICE

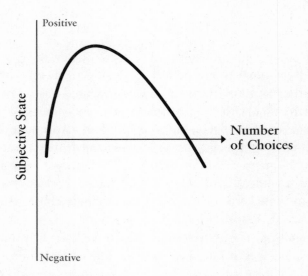

One would think that given this paradox, the right thing for technology companies to do would be to reduce the amount of choice that is available to us. Yet, search results stretch on for thousands of pages and social media feeds are infinite.

Growth is the primary driver for these companies. Having the widest choice attracts the most people, just like in Iyengar and Lepper's experiment. We are drawn to novel information. 'Stickiness' can be solved using other 'growth hacks' such as recommendations, personalization and social feeds.

In fact, recommendation technologies would be meaningless if we didn't have too much choice in the first place. We wouldn't need gatekeepers, rating scores and algorithms if the amount of content were manageable. Too much choice is what keeps us coming back for more, hoping that luck will be in our favour this time and we will discover something surprising or exciting. Too much choice is why we let autoplay decide our next video. If we give people too much choice and the option to let the machine decide for them, most will prefer to not exert self-control and handover the reins to the machine.

Too much choice obfuscates the most meaningful choice—our choice to stop.

#3 THINKING IS HARD

We've all either said it ourselves or heard someone else say, 'my head hurts to think about that'.

Cognitive effort is known to be hard. Scientists from McGill University, Canada, set up an experiment to ask people to choose between a cognitively demanding task or experience painful heat. In their results published in 2020, they conclude,

> 'This provides compelling evidence that cognitive effort is aversive and the desire to avoid it can be quite strong. Put simply, people preferred to experience physical pain rather than do something mentally demanding. In fact, participants made effort-avoidant choices even when faced with the maximum ethically permissible pain level: on average, participants accepted the painful stimulation, calibrated to 80/100 (100 = "extremely intense" pain), approximately 28 per cent of the time to avoid performing the cognitively difficult 4-back task.'

The resistance to cognitive effort varies across individuals, but all of us show some degree of resistance. We can overcome it, but doing so feels tiring. When we're stressed, distracted or tired, we're less likely to think about our own best interests and do what's mentally easy instead. Even if the mentally easy option involves physical pain.

Aversion to thinking too hard makes us take all sorts of decisions that may not be in our favour. We click the button to accept all cookies because it is coloured a familiar blue. We don't uncheck the box next to 'sign me up for marketing communications' because it is selected by default. Not wanting to think is also why habits are so successful. Familiar pathways of action are the ones of least resistance for our brains.

In 2014, in a popular book called *Hooked: How to Build Habit-Forming Products*, Nir Eyal lays out the process for piggybacking on this fundamental human trait to make apps addictive. The mechanism for hooking users is simple—present users with a trigger, and if they act on that trigger, reward them. But there is a secret ingredient. On his website, the author advises businesses, 'At the heart of the Hook Model is a powerful cognitive quirk described by B.F. Skinner, in the 1950s, called a variable schedule of rewards.'

The famous psychologist B.F. Skinner proved that you could teach animals seemingly intelligent behaviours by reinforcing desired behaviours with rewards. In a very popular video, Skinner uses reinforcement to teach a pigeon to make a complete turn. He does this in under a minute. The 'cognitive quirk' that Eyal mentions is that something strange happens when you make the rewards unpredictable. Skinner demonstrated that variable rewards resulted in most instances of the desired behaviour. It also led to behaviours that were the hardest to extinguish. Skinner compares this effect to a slot machine in a casino. He says that the uncertainty of rewards makes each iteration of the desired behaviour like a spin of the slot machine. For the subject, the desired behaviour can become as addictive as a slot machine.

The reason we find it so hard to look away from our phones is the same as the reasons for which we procrastinate. It is an emotion-regulation problem. Instead of doing what we know we should, we perform an easier, automatic and familiar behaviour to avoid the task. It could be scrolling through social media, catching up on

Think about the last time that you were in one of those rabbit holes.

Say you decided to check out your favourite distraction. It could be a news site, social media, streaming video or something else. Each link you clicked, feed you scrolled or the recommended video you watched; all of these pushed you into automatic, fast and continuous behaviours. You probably lost more time to them than you wanted. You were in the zone.

But what made you open the distracting app in the first place?

The likely answer is that you open it out of force of habit in the moments between finishing a task and starting another. You probably even know what important thing you should do next, but your brain pushes back on exerting self-control. You feel a sense of discomfort that manifests either as boredom or anxiety. That is when you seek the zone.

In the past, when you felt this discomfort, you may have decided to comfort yourself by opening one of these apps. The infinite choices offered by these apps never give you a sense of completion, so you keep going. Each scroll, refresh or click gives you new content that may or may not be useful, just like the slot machine's variable rewards. These continuous, fast and variable rewards take you into the zone. You're able to avoid thinking about whatever anxiety that triggered you to use the app because you're in the zone.

From the brain's perspective, this action actually resolves the task. We were facing discomfort in anticipation of the task. When we avoid the task and are in the zone, we don't feel anything. Our brains now associate reaching for our phones as the solution to all such discomfort. Over our millions of interactions with our phones, we've repeated this behaviour enough for it to become a habit. The apps have managed to train us to associate the cue of discomfort with the behaviour of picking up our phone like Skinner trained pigeons. We reach for the apps or news feeds that make us lose a sense of space and time.

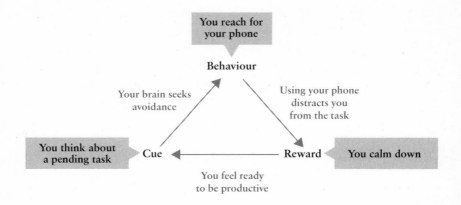

Why you lose time to your phone

Eventually, one would get bored of any slot machine and stop. But, our computers and smartphones are portals to multiple slot machines. Moreover, there are no boundaries between these apps and browser tabs. We end up moving from one virtual slot machine to another, chasing the zone.

The next time you find yourself losing time as Dhruv did, ask if you were truly present in what you were doing, or if you were simply chasing the zone. All of us indulge in this escapist behaviour sometimes. But our devices can make this escapism into an insidious habit. And the habits that have been reinforced millions of times by our daily actions become very hard to break.

People often frame their phone-addiction problem in terms of what they do on the phone. People believe they are addicted to Twitter or Instagram or YouTube. The real problem is not *what* they use, but *when* they use their phones. We've trained ourselves to reach for our phones in response to an unpleasant emotion. We seek to get into the zone so that we don't have to face these difficult emotions.

Unlearning this deeply ingrained habit is going to take time and effort. It will involve changing many behaviours that are now automatic and easy. Often, we fail in our attempts because the challenge is vast, and we're seeking quick and easy answers.

The most toxic answer is that you simply need to do better.

WILLPOWER

One half of our toxic relationship with technology is due to our own lack of self-control. Surely, if we managed to exercise our willpower better, we could stop ourselves from getting into the zone and losing time?

While this approach sounds correct, it misses a critical point.

Runners and athletes often describe a similar experience of being in the zone and losing a sense of time when they are fully engaged in their sport. Our digital slot machines are designed to be engaging, but often when we lose time to them, we feel guilt and shame. Now imagine if you spent an hour being in the zone, but while running. You are likely to feel happy and fulfilled. The difference is primarily that when we are lost on our phones, we are *unintentionally* in the zone. Whereas, when we are running, we are *intentionally* looking to be in the state of singular focus. The problem isn't that we chase the zone but that we spend our time in zones that we do not intend to.

It is the gap between our intention and our attention that makes us unhappy. As we've said before, the goal of *bitfulness* isn't to spend less time on our phones. It is to spend time better.

Hence, depending on our willpower alone is a bad strategy. Not being able to exert sufficient self-control is how we developed these behaviours in the first place. Relying on willpower alone is like trying to quit smoking while carrying a cigarette packet with you wherever you go—you can exert self-control on most days, but sooner or later, you will have a moment of weakness and reach for that packet.

The real problem is that our technology usage is often designed around who we wish we were, not who we are.

We wish we were someone who only looks at their phone when necessary. We wish we were not easily distracted and always made healthy choices. We wish that we only checked messages and emails when convenient to us, and not compulsively. We wish that we only used social media for entertainment and not scroll through it mindlessly. In reality, we are capable of focusing but often slip up. We are ambitious and conscientious but also prone to procrastination and laziness. Apps and platforms exploit this gap between our self-image and our reality.

Our self-image of being a conscientious, rational and motivated human being only gets in the way of fixing our relationship with technology. Instead of fixing the causes of toxic behaviour, we try to exercise more self-control on its symptoms and fail. We blame ourselves for not being capable enough or strong enough to change. We've been tricked into believing that because we have the choice to switch off, not being able to switch off is a *personal* failing. This belief is both untrue and unhelpful.

When it comes to addiction, we tend to focus on two things—the addict and the substance. There is a third factor we often fail to consider—our environment.

In 1971, the US military noted that 15 per cent of American soldiers in Vietnam were heroin addicts. Heroin is extremely addictive, and few thought there was a chance for these soldiers to be de-addicted. But, when these soldiers reached home, the statistics were astonishing. Less than 5 per cent of the soldiers relapsed in the first year, and less than 12 per cent in three years. Scientists had to challenge their current understanding of addiction.

The basis for deciding if a substance is addictive was tests carried out on laboratory rats who were isolated in small cages with two drips that they could choose from. One drip usually contained water or food, and the other contained addictive substances such as morphine or cocaine. What most of those studies showed is that rats would obsessively choose the drugs over food or water, and if they were allowed to, many would overdose.

Canadian psychologist Bruce K. Alexander set up a series of experiments in the late 1970s to see if changing the environment that the rats were in would change their behaviour. So, he designed a rat park—a space with 200 times the floor area of a regular experiment cage. Other than the usual two drips, it contained a play area, food, and most importantly, other rats to socialize with. Alexander demonstrated that rats in this environment rarely chose the drugs. Even those that did never overdosed. Surprisingly, even the same rats that would obsessively choose drugs in the solitary cages would wean off their habit once they were introduced into the rat park.

It is not simply the neurochemistry of our brain interacting with the substance. It is also our environment and our social context. When the soldiers came back to the very different environment of their homes, or rats came to the rat park, even the most deeply ingrained habits learned on the battlefield could be overcome.

The way to practise *bitfulness* is, therefore, awareness-driven habit and environment change. In Part Two of this book, we will thoughtfully design our extended mind. Instead of exercising willpower, make it *easier* to stay in context, minimize choices and reinforce good habits. If we design our environment around who we are, instead of who we wish we were, we can guide ourselves towards making healthier choices automatically.

There are no tricks that will help you unlearn these toxic habits overnight. Our focus isn't on eliminating all toxic habits. Instead, we will focus on fixing our relationship with technology by creating tiny good habits. We will design our extended minds to make these good habits automatic. Some of these environmental changes will help these habits stick instantly, and some may need tweaking. Bit by bit, we can reset our relationship with technology.

Remember, it does take two to make a toxic relationship. This chapter only covered how we contribute to the toxic patterns of behaviours. In the next chapter, we will learn how our technology contributes to this toxicity.

3

THE PROBLEM WITH IT

THE THIRD CRISIS

Our relationship with technology was not always toxic.

The first personal computers were to be used the way personal calculators were—as tools to support an individual's thought process. The internet changed this thinking tool into a gateway. Your extended mind has unrestricted access to a vast amount of information through a global network. The flip-side is that the global network has unrestricted access to your mind too. Businesses soon realized that the internet is the most cost-effective way to reach their customers and grab their attention.

The internet, thus, hijacked our extended minds. Our technology is no longer a bicycle to help our mind ride to its destination. Instead, the internet tends to opt us into rowing someone else's galley. Rather than technology helping us achieve our goals, we seem to be helping technology achieve *its* goals.

The internet has changed the fundamental logic of personal information technologies. Not just our phones, but also our refrigerators, TVs, lights and microwaves are becoming 'smart' by connecting to the internet. Once connected, businesses hope to extract something of value from us continuously—whether it's our money, attention or data.

On the other end of the equation, the internet has changed the fundamental logic of businesses too. Online companies have to build their businesses in a very different way from offline companies. The capital and resources available to them make them favour massive speed and scale. The business logic driving these companies is affecting their relationships with their users.

Our individual relationship with our technology turning toxic is only a symptom of a much deeper crisis facing humanity. The internet, as it is today, is not capable of making everything in society digital, while still upholding the values we want our society to protect. We can already see some fault lines start to emerge as people begin to question the role of social media in our protests and our elections. If we continue building the internet this way, we risk an existential crisis.

Humanity is already facing two major crises in the physical world with pandemics and climate change. There is a third crisis brewing in our digital world.

This digital crisis combines the worst aspects of humanity's other two global crises. It is exponential in its spread like a pandemic, and its immediate convenience masks its more long-term harmful effects like the climate crisis. It may also cause economic and social damage in the long run, even as we all think our individual lives are getting better in the short run.

We'd still rate the internet, unequivocally, good. Overall, building an open, decentralized, digital communication network that connects everyone has been one of humanity's greatest achievements. The Third Crisis is not that we are going digital.

The Third Crisis is that *how* we are going digital will lead to an imbalance of power in society.

To understand this crisis, its causes and its consequences, we have to go back to how the internet hijacked our extended minds. It all started with the internet's original sin.

THE ORIGINAL SIN

In 1989, Sir Timothy Berners-Lee, also known as TBL, was frustrated by not being able to find the right files, so he invented the World Wide Web.

Established in 1954, the European Organization for Nuclear Research, also known as CERN, is a research organization based in

Geneva. It operates the largest particle physics laboratory in the world. Due to the size of the project, thousands of scientists collaborate at CERN. As an organization, it probably generates the most amount of scientific data and knowledge in the world. However, TBL invented the WWW because CERN was also losing a lot of that knowledge.

Many scientists would join CERN for research purposes for some duration and leave. As a result, a lot of the knowledge about their work and research would leave with them. CERN enjoyed access to the internet, but this was the internet of 1989. It connected computers into one universal network. But it wasn't very helpful in knowing what was on those computers.

Inside the computers, people organized documents according to their own specific hierarchies. Searches only worked if two people used the same keyword for the same thing. Even though the knowledge was all on one network, it wasn't usable yet.

So Berners-Lee decided that he'd change the way people shared knowledge. Instead of using the traditional hierarchical approach of files and folders, TBL was inspired by a technological idea called hypertext. In 1990, he created an open standard called the Hypertext Markup Language (HTML) and the first browser to parse HTML, WorldWideWeb. According to the world's first-ever website, still hosted at info.cern.ch:

> The WorldWideWeb (W3) is a wide-area hypermedia information retrieval initiative aiming to give universal access to a large universe of documents.

Berners-Lee had created a way to decouple information from the computer on which it sat. Instead of saying 'I want a file from this folder on that computer', the web allows you to say 'I want the file residing at this URL'. The browser's job is to decode that URL, i.e., Uniform Resource Locator, to locate an actual file somewhere on a server on the internet, retrieve it and display it to you.

The biggest innovation of hypertext was hyperlinks. Imagine how much harder Wikipedia would be to use if there were no links and you had to navigate to each page by digging through a folder tree. Webpages and weblinks allowed the connections between two files to be contextual. They made finding the right information considerably easier than the old files and folder system.

Though painfully bland by today's standards, TBL's invention was path-breaking for its time. The internet has existed in some form since 1969, but it was the World Wide Web in 1990 that kicked off the storm. In 1991, the internet became accessible to the public. The internet was still a public good, a garden of Eden where interesting people came together to share interesting things. A group of academicians and others formed a not-for-profit to govern the newly born web's specifications.

Around 1992, the web started attracting more hobbyists and entrepreneurs. The internet was seen as a platform with infinite possibilities. One person it inspired was the then twenty-two-year-old student Marc Andreessen. Andreessen created the Mosaic browser at the National Center for Supercomputing Applications, a largely government-funded research centre based out of the University of Illinois at Urbana–Champaign.

Mosaic was one of the first browsers which would add images inline to the web. Mosaic wanted the web to be more than just an elite research tool. They made the browsing experience as accessible as possible, and as a result, Mosaic spread like wildfire. Marc Andreessen eventually graduated, left the NCSA, launched Netscape Navigator as a private corporation, and ended up barefoot on *TIME* magazine's cover. Thus, marking the beginning of the internet revolution.

In 1994, the web reached an inflexion point where the popularity and reach of the internet had begun to outpace the architects who helped create its foundations. Entrepreneurs on the internet wanted to get paid for what they were building. But the internet had no inherent way of letting them collect money. The sceptics had begun to ask if the internet could sustain real businesses or if it was just hype.

One of the artefacts to have gained mainstream cultural popularity from the internet is the 404 error, i.e., 'page not found'. Fewer people know about the 402 error, i.e., 'payment required'. The web creators had imagined that the web would be a peer-to-peer technology, and people would trade with each other directly over the web through micropayments. The web creators wrote the '402' error as a to-do to themselves—an error code reserved for a future when people could pay each other directly for content.

An internet native micropayments system never got built. Instead of waiting for the technology that enabled payments on the internet, internet entrepreneurs got around this inconvenience by changing their business model.

On 27 October 1994, the online magazine hotwired.co.uk found a solution to this missing infrastructure—displaying the first banner ad.

Advertising meant that new internet companies did not have to wait for the technology to collect pennies from millions of customers. Instead, they could collect cheques worth thousands of dollars from a handful of advertisers. Advertising also helps reach more users since the content can be made free. Given the lack of payment technology, choosing advertising as a business model makes perfect sense. The early web entrepreneurs couldn't have known that taking a bite of the juicy advertising apple would eventually lead to the loss of the internet's innocence. This moment is now considered by many to be the one when the internet went from a collective project to being a commercial project.

In an article in *The Atlantic* in 2014, Ethan Zuckerman, the creator of the pop-up ad, called this moment the internet's *original sin*.

TARGETING

All advertising has a particular weakness, best articulated over a hundred years ago by department store magnate John Wanamaker: 'Half the money I spend on advertising is wasted; the trouble is I don't know which half.'

When it began, advertising on the internet did not look very different from advertising on billboards. It was a large banner designed to capture your attention as you went around surfing the web on your own business. Marketers soon realized the internet is not a billboard. It didn't take long before someone asked, 'Why are we showing the same ads to everybody who visits our site?' If you were surfing an article about cars, wouldn't it make sense to show you an ad about cars? If you were reading an article about books, wouldn't it make more sense to offer you an ad about books instead of cars? Thus, ads began to be targeted based on the content and context of the web page.

The internet promised to answer Wanamaker's question. You could find out how many people saw the ad, how many clicks your ads were getting, etc. Getting data this fast was very unusual for marketers in the 1990s. Until that point, a campaign cycle would take weeks to plan and execute. Feedback would only arrive in a quarter or two when the sales results came in. Online advertising was the first taste of data for advertisers, and they would soon get hungry for more.

In 1996, DoubleClick was launched. This online ad agency changed the way marketers thought about their jobs and would go on to be acquired in 2007 for an eye-popping US$3.1 billion, all in cash, by Google. In the late 1990s, though, DoubleClick was still a small operation. Through early tracking technologies, they were able to tell their clients what ads people saw and when. Essentially, data on ad *performance*. It wasn't long before advertisers realized they could target even better if they started asking who exactly is watching these ads.

That is, data on *people*.

Targeted advertising is a seductive idea. If you've ever had to sell anything, you would know that getting people to part with their money is hard. But what if you could put your product in front of those exact people who are looking for something like it? This part-oracle, part-cupid matching of seekers and sellers is the ultimate promise of all online advertising firms. They collect data to help target ads to the customers who are likely to buy them. In theory, a win-win!

Targeted advertising is, hence, a lucrative industry. Companies such as Google, Facebook, and others match ads with viewers at great scale and speed. Global spending on digital advertising was roughly US$333 billion in 2019, i.e., 50 per cent of all advertising spend globally. It is still growing.

Information wants to be free, but it still costs money to deliver it. Advertising makes the internet accessible to everyone, claim its supporters. Google could serve us all of the world's information for free in exchange for a few ads. Facebook connects you to all your friends in return for a few sponsored posts. The web allows us to create more information than ever, cheaper than ever. What's the harm with tacking on a little more information on behalf of an advertiser, if it pays the bill?

Nobel prize-winning economist Herbert Simon saw things differently. 'What information consumes is rather obvious: it consumes the attention of its recipients. Hence, a wealth of information creates a poverty of attention.' If you think this is an accurate description of the internet, it is worth mentioning that Simon said this in 1971.

The advertising model made attention the real currency of the internet. Selling targeted ads was how companies encashed your attention. Targeting is why AdTech companies like collecting user data. Data helps match users to advertisers.

In effect, the lack of payments infrastructure on the early web has led us to our current attention and data-hungry internet.

WINNERS, TECH, ALL

We're facing the Third Crisis today because there was a vacuum at the core of the internet.

David D. Clark, head of the Internet Architecture Board through most of the 1980s, recalls this exchange with an unnamed economist in his book, *Designing an Internet*.

> *Economist*: The internet is about routing money. Routing packets is a side effect. You screwed up the money routing protocols.
>
> *Clark*: I did not design any money routing protocols!
>
> *Economist*: That's what I said.

As there weren't any 'money routing protocols', individuals couldn't transact with each other without an intermediary to facilitate this transaction. Entrepreneurs and Venture Capitalists (VCs) saw an opportunity in this flaw. Online businesses could become these intermediaries for everyone on the internet.

With the help of plentiful capital, entrepreneurs started inventing and evolving ever-faster ways to make money on the internet. In the early internet days, it became clear that online businesses need not have a natural ceiling the way other offline businesses had. Costco could have a great business model, but if it didn't have a store in your area, it didn't matter. But amazon.com could be accessed by anyone, anywhere. Amazon could become bigger than Costco while incurring fewer brick & mortar costs.

Becoming big also triggered another positive feedback loop. As more people started transacting on the web, they would now look to the existing, trusted big brands on the web, such as Amazon. And if you already had many sellers on your platform, your platform was better than the competition. Any early leads you get serve as a barrier to your competition. Entrepreneurs understood that as opposed to the cautious strategies of building offline businesses, online businesses were about speed and scale. The biggest would also be most likely to keep getting bigger, faster.

A lot of investors poured money into the dot-com boom of the mid to late 1990s. Even the *Wall Street Journal* advised personal investors to 'rethink' the 'quaint idea' of profits and take an interest in internet stocks. Common slogans popular between entrepreneurs and investors in the late 1990s are simply blunter versions of what we hear today. They included 'get big fast' or 'get large or get lost'.

Although the dot-com bubble burst, the investors were unlucky, not incorrect. The internet business models they were betting on were winner-take-all by design. They attracted a lot of capital because once the dust settled, the eventual winner would have a very stable hold over the market—a virtual monopoly. Once a sufficiently large player emerges, most investors would stop putting capital into alternatives. The competition would get wiped out because the big tend to get bigger, and the smaller ones shrink to zero. None of this was illegal. It was simply uncharted territory.

This fundamental winner-take-all logic is still how we fund and build internet businesses today. VCs explicitly want to fund online businesses with a 'moat'. That is a fundamental systematic advantage in their design, which is a legal but difficult barrier for the competition to overcome. Once VCs fund companies, they encourage them to burn money to become unicorns. That is, 'get big or get lost', but phrased in more contemporary terms such as 'blitzscaling'. Companies start focusing on improving the product, solving consumer problems, offering adjacent services, etc. to scale.

But this focus on scale is also how the toxic patterns begin. Many companies start making tweaks to increase their metrics. These tweaks, like autoplay or infinite feeds, do lead to an increase in our usage. But, increased usage is not always in line with the user's goals. The increased usage isn't always from free will, and could sometimes be from addiction.

We, the authors, have spent nearly the entirety of our careers in the space of information technology and related policy. Despite the thirty-four-year difference in our ages, we share a sense of wonder and excitement in what information technology has achieved and continues to achieve. For both of us, the internet has been a fantastic opportunity to learn and connect with wonderful people. It is full of exciting problems to work on. We're both optimistic that the answer to society's problems lies in more, not less, technology.

Optimism is not the same as naivety. Our excitement about technology is specifically about humanity's increasing ability to do marvellous things. Using that ability to benefit *all* of society is another challenge altogether. Our current, winner-take-all internet does not meet this challenge.

Although the internet started as an open and decentralized network in the 1980s, private companies have built most of our modern web over the last three decades. The original creators of the internet may have laid the foundation with an open communications network. But, we've outsourced building the rest of our internet infrastructure to players building walled gardens.

Companies such as Facebook, Google, Amazon or other such large tech companies are large because they each fulfil an essential function on the web. Facebook is how we communicate with our social networks. Google has built an index of the web. Amazon has created the largest marketplace. They are all digital infrastructure, and in the pursuit of market share growth, they have all been designed to be winner-take-all.

A handful of tech companies effectively own the roads and highways of the digital world. We are looking at a future in which these companies are not just the winners of their own markets but also have the power to decide who wins in all adjacent markets. For example, the online travel industry alleges that Google favoured its own hotel and flight booking products in search results. Amazon has been accused of propping up its own brands on its marketplace search results. Uber drivers are often protesting about how the company's fare policies work against the drivers' interests.

Tech companies maintain they are acting in the users' best interests, but their competitors see an unfair advantage in their ability to change search results or set prices. Even without those systematic advantages, competing with these giants is challenging because of the vast resources they have now amassed. In April 2020, the top five tech companies alone were sitting on US$555 billion in cash and cash equivalents. These companies have achieved their dominant position by genuinely building innovative products and giving users what they want. Just because they have near-monopoly power doesn't automatically imply they will abuse it.

But the question to ask ourselves is why even afford them the chance?

The original internet had a simple idea built into its design. The network that connected everyone was not to be controlled by any single one. The internet belonged to everyone and no one. This is not a radical decision. The precursor to the internet was built as a defence research project by a collaboration of scientists across many universities. In a few years, development of the technology moved to academia. The time and effort that went into the internet was essentially funded by public institutions, i.e., by all of us. It is hardly surprising that the output of the combined efforts of thousands of scientists and engineers, funded by public money, was a technology that belonged to all of us.

Our current internet infrastructure looks very different from what the internet was supposed to be. Instead of belonging to all of us, critical parts of the internet are under the control of a few players. Internet companies gloss over this difference because they maintain that what's good for the user is good for the business. In the presence of alternatives, customers will choose the product that serves their needs well, and affordably. This is true when the control over the infrastructure is used to help users achieve their goals. However, it is when user goals and the platform's goals misalign, that we should be worried about their power.

In 1998, two graduate students, funded by a public grant, wrote a paper talking about this problem in the context of search engines. 'The goals of the advertising business model do not always correspond to providing quality search to users,' they wrote. 'We expect that advertising funded search engines will be inherently biased towards the advertisers and away from the needs of the consumers.'

Who had this foresight in 1998? Sergei Brin and Larry Page, the co-founders of Google.

We do not doubt that the people who start, or work at internet firms are honest individuals trying to do good. But as they say, the road to hell is paved with good intentions. The issues we have today with the internet—misinformation, loss of privacy, losing attention, increase in polarization, election meddling, etc.—are all questions around the design of our digital infrastructure, and hence, are all questions about control over our digital infrastucture. The imbalance of power over critical infrastructure is not amenable to an equal or just future.

Regulations can check some excesses of internet companies, but they can't resolve the fundamental paradox created by private infrastructure. If we continue funding and building the internet the way we currently do, we risk upsetting not just our livelihoods and our economy but all of our major societal institutions. While we can learn how to manage ourselves better and practise *bitfulness,* we also need to fix the underlying problem in our relationship with technology.

We need to rebuild our digital roads and highways in the way we build our regular roads and highways—designed to serve us and not for us to serve them.

WORKING TOGETHER

Disease is as old as humans, but pandemics are a side-effect of civilization. The COVID-19 virus may have originated in a single city in China, but our transport and logistics networks made the new disease a global pandemic. Even the Black Plague, which killed approximately a quarter of the population in the fourteenth century, was spread from port city to port city by rats travelling on merchant ships. Our transportation network also leads to increased fossil fuel consumption and climate change. Every time humans have created networked technologies, we have created a new class of complex problems.

When it comes to the other two existential crises facing humanity, we have a reasonable plan to address problems emerging from our technology, even if it is hard to follow.

During the pandemic, in just a few days, we figured out that to prevent catching COVID-19, people must wash their hands, wear a mask, maintain a minimum distance of six feet, and avoid unventilated rooms. For climate change, we know that we must move to cleaner fuels, minimize consumption of plastic, eat less meat, travel less and by foot where possible. These are simple measures that we can all take to lessen the problem.

These individual solutions, however, help manage, not eliminate, the problem. To end a pandemic, we need collective action. We need countries to invest in testing and health infrastructure, develop and administer vaccines, implement better pandemic preparation plans, among other measures. To fix climate change, we need better policies such as carbon taxes, clean air legislation, better monitoring of pollution, promotion of renewable energy, and other big ideas.

Every new global technology creates problems, but our history demonstrates we can solve those problems if we coordinate and cooperate. Our most recent progress on vaccines for the COVID-19 pandemic shows us what we can do if we are willing to do what it takes and do it together.

The internet is the first technology to connect everyone and give everyone a voice. It is connecting people who have never coordinated before. There are bound to be complex problems that emerge as this technology becomes widely adopted. We do not call the internet's missing infrastructure a crisis to make it sound graver than it is. We call it a crisis because it affects all of us, and like any crisis, it will require collective action to fix. In the absence of our collective will, our digital infrastructure become walled gardens. We have some freedom but no control over the design of the infrastructure itself. As more of our lives become digital, the power over this infrastructure will equate with power over all dimensions of our lives. We need to reach a consensus on what our digital infrastructure should look like and what values it should protect. In Part Three of this book, we cover what we can do to solve The Third Crisis collectively.

Before we do that, we're going to start by fixing our individual relationship with our technology. We want to restore a sense of calm and control in how we use our devices. In Part Two of the book, we go over some specific strategies to reclaim our time, attention and privacy. We also cover the principles that guide them so that you can adapt these ideas to your own personal situation.

Ultimately, these principles represent a simple truth—if you don't design your technology around your life, someone else will design your life around their technology. If you want to control your time, attention, and privacy, you will need more than just willpower or quick hacks.

You need *a system*.

PART TWO

THE INDIVIDUAL

4

HOW TO BE BITFUL

A QUIET MIND

In 1972, Timothy Gallwey, a college administrator and part-time tennis coach, wrote a book that would change how all professional athletes trained. Instead of teaching stances, grips, swings or other technical details of tennis, the book called the *Inner Game of Tennis* focused entirely on what happens inside a player's mind.

Gallwey believes that most people need to stop *consciously trying* to play well and instead *quieten the mind*. Our mind places obstacles between us and our best performance in the form of self-doubt, criticism and lapses in concentration. We all have an inner critic, telling us how we're failing or that we need to do better. Allowing these thoughts to take over can dampen any player's performance. A quiet mind silences the inner critic. It allows our subconscious to focus exclusively on playing and not on judging how we played. Hence, Gallwey believes that the most important skill for good tennis is relaxed concentration.

He offers a slightly unsportsmanlike method to test his theory.

The next time you are playing an opponent having a 'hot streak', Gallwey suggests you ask them, 'What are you doing so differently that's making your forehand so good today?' Most will acknowledge the compliment and take your question sincerely. They will reply with how they are swinging or meeting the ball in front and other such

43

details. When you get back to the game, your compliment is likely to do more damage than any insult. Your opponent will try to follow their own advice. Their mind is now paying attention to the very things they advised you about. Their effortless hot streak will falter as they try to put conscious effort into their shots.

The ideas in Gallwey's book were groundbreaking for their time. The role of psychology in sports performance hadn't gained mainstream popularity when the book was first released. The first *Journal of Sports Psychology* was published only in 1979. The 1984 Olympics would see the first sports psychologists travel with some of the teams. By the next Olympics, most teams had multiple of them. Gallwey's book clearly articulated what every professional sports team would soon realize: 'The opponent within your own head is more daunting than the one on the other side of the net.'

Gallwey's observation is just as valid outside the tennis court. The publishers had expected this niche book to sell maybe 20,000 copies to budding tennis players. The book has sold over a million copies, not only to athletes from all disciplines but also business leaders, musicians and anyone else trying to improve at something. None of these other readers wanted to learn about tennis. They wanted to learn about *the mental state of relaxed concentration* that allows one to excel at anything.

Unsurprisingly, scientists have since then given this mental state a name and studied it extensively. In 1996, Mihaly Csikszentmihalyi wrote the seminal book on this mental state titled Flow. He describes 'flow' as a mental state in which a person performing an activity is fully immersed in a feeling of *energized focus*, *full involvement* and *enjoyment* in the process of the activity.

All of us have experienced flow.

Whether in sports, at work or in pursuit of a hobby, we have had the experience of being fully immersed in an activity. We have full concentration on the task at hand. We lose a sense of time and place. Action and awareness merge, and making the next move is effortless. We don't need external motivation to continue. Our minds naturally quieten, and we are intensely focused yet relaxed.

If the Flow mental state sounds familiar, it is because it describes exactly The Zone from Chapter 2. Natasha Dow Schüll, the author of *Addiction By Design*, claims that the designs of slot machines naturally lend themselves to this flow-like state where players lose a sense of time and place. The two states are indistinguishable in their effects on us. The only difference lies in the alignment of our intention and attention.

Gallwey's fundamental insight is as relevant to our screens as it is to sports. If we are *trying* to spend less time on our screens or forcing ourselves to be productive, we are not unlike the tennis player on a 'hot streak' reminded of their forehand. Our conscious effort only makes it harder to actually do our best.

The more daunting opponent is within your own head. Self-doubt, self-judgement and other negative emotions get in the way of our best work. Our minds seek refuge from these unpleasant emotions and often find it in the distractions on our devices. Over time, these toxic patterns get reinforced and solidify.

Instead of giving in to these patterns, we need to learn the art of *bitfulness*.

HOW TO BE BITFUL

Most of us think of our devices in the same way in which we think of hammers.

We see our technology as a tool that we use to get things done. As the old adage has taught us, a bad workman always blames his tools. Being good workmen, when we are unable to focus, we blame ourselves instead. We think the solution to our problems is to concentrate harder. We use willpower to direct our minds to focus on the task. If we have a focused mind, we will be better operators of our tools.

This model puts the cart before the horse.

Yes, we operate our phones as tools, but the relationship isn't one way. These tools affect us deeply in a way that no hammer ever can. An experiment was conducted with 800 smartphone users by Professor Adrian Ward from University of Texas. In the experiment, people were randomly divided into groups where one group had to keep their phones on their desks, face down. Another group had to keep their phones in their pockets or bags, but out of sight. The third group of people were asked to leave their phones in another room during the tests. In all three groups, some were asked to turn off their phones.

The participants were then given tasks that needed cognitive effort. Even though all participants reported giving their full focus and attention to the task at hand, the participants whose phones were in the other room *significantly* outperformed those whose smartphones were on them.

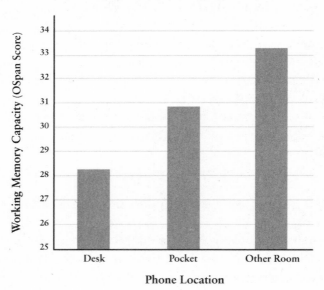

Simply having your phone in the same room
can significantly reduce your capacity to think

It didn't even matter if those who had their phones had turned them off. If the phones were near or on them, their capacities diminished.

'We see a linear trend that suggests that as the smartphone becomes more noticeable, the participants' available cognitive capacity decreases,' Ward said. 'Your conscious mind isn't thinking about your smartphone, but that process—the process of requiring yourself to not think about something—uses up some of your limited cognitive resources. It's a brain drain.'

In the internet age, our devices are more than just tools. Our devices don't merely connect to the internet. They also represent our connection to the world. A large part of our social interactions now happen through these devices. Your acceptance letter for college, that email about your promotion, the texts from your partner, the results of your blood test, the graphs showing whether your investments are going up or down—our phones are the physical manifestation of all this information that affects us deeply. As Professor Ward discovered, simply the *presence* of a smartphone is enough to reduce cognitive capacity as we try not to check it.

Now imagine the ability of your phone to affect your mental and emotional states when you are looking at it. We use our devices to get things done, but our devices are also *doing things to us*.

Our attempts to spend less time on our personal distractions often fail because we fail to consider the two-way nature of this relationship.

We look at restricting screen time the way we look at restricting calories—as an act of self-deprivation. Trying to restrict screen time requires us to constantly exert willpower against our desire to pick up our phones and check in on the things we care and worry about. Exerting willpower is already hard but it becomes harder when we're fixating on a negative rule that deprives us. Trying to not use your phone is like trying to not think of an elephant. The more you think about NOT doing something, the harder it becomes to NOT do it.

Instead, we need to focus our energy on a different but positive rule. We need to pay attention to the quality of the time we spend on our screens rather than its quantity.

Each time we use our devices, we access them in one of two modes. Either we can use them mindfully— in flow, focused on what we want to do, or we can use them as an escape—mindlessly chasing the 'zone' to avoid doing what we should do.

We think of *bitfulness* as the ability to spend our time on our devices *better*. Specifically, we want to focus on making sure that the time we spend with our devices is mindful and aligned with our intentions. We understand that advising someone who is struggling with focus to be more mindful is akin to asking someone feeling low to be happier instead.

The hard part is not knowing *what* to do but *how* to do it.

The next eight chapters of this book deal with the how. We cover practical strategies to spend time on our devices mindfully and quieten the inner critic. But to help us bridge the gap between knowing *what* to do and knowing *how* to do it, it is useful to understand *why* these strategies help.

The art of *bitfulness* comes down to three fundamental principles.

1. Mirrors, not Windows
2. Don't swim upstream
3. Define our selves

In the rest of this chapter, we explore what each of these means.

MIRRORS, NOT WINDOWS

Being mindful means being aware.

Specifically, it means being aware of one's own state of mind without judgement. When we are aware of our state of mind, we can make calm decisions rather than react emotionally. Using our devices mindfully doesn't mean having to be a zen monk and detaching from the worldly pleasure of our devices. It also doesn't imply that we will never end up wasting time on our devices. Being mindful allows us to step away from our usual frame to see our context, thoughts, emotions and actions in perspective.

It means that the next time we catch ourselves scrolling aimlessly, we won't jump to conclusions like 'I am useless because I always procrastinate' or 'This app is addictive and hence I waste time.' Instead, being mindful means you can reflect and ask, 'Why did I choose to scroll rather than do X?'. Answering that question honestly holds a much better chance of fixing our problems than any 'hack'.

Science tells us that the most likely answer to why we procrastinate lies in our emotions.

As we said before, procrastination is not a time-management problem; it is an emotion-regulation problem. Dr Fuschia Sirois, professor of psychology at the University of Sheffield, says, 'People engage in this irrational cycle of chronic procrastination because of an inability to manage negative moods around a task.' The cycle goes like this:

You think about doing a task. Your brain projects into the future and imagines what doing the task will feel like. Your brain predicts that doing this task will generate a negative mood. This prediction of a future negative mood puts you in a negative mood right now, often causing us to avoid and delay the task.

The reasons for negative moods around a task may be many. It could be that the task is boring or inherently unpleasant, like scrubbing the toilet. A lot of people put off making their will, even though it is both easy and critical because it involves thinking about the unpleasant idea of their own death. Another reason for a negative mood could also be that the task triggers deeper feelings of insecurity, low self-esteem, self-doubt or other anxieties. For example, someone may be delaying updating their resume because they have a latent fear of being rejected. In every case, our brains avoid the potential negative mood by avoiding doing the task altogether.

Feeling a mixture of emotions around a task is not unnatural. If anything, it probably means you care about what you're doing and are invested in getting it right. We can't and don't have to change how we feel about a task.

What we need to change are the toxic patterns of behaviour we've learnt with our devices when we encounter those emotions.

Whenever we feel these emotions, we reach for our phone or switch to a new tab and seek escape. Reinforcement over the hundreds of times we touch our phone every day means that this pattern is an almost automatic habit. We may open the offending app mindlessly before we even realize that we have.

The Third Crisis is further aggravating our toxic relationship. Internet businesses need our attention to sustain. The logic of their business model means that our devices are configured to nudge us toward these windows of escape. Wherever we are, whenever we like, our phones act as portals to other worlds. This can be a useful property sometimes, but not when we're procrastinating. Since procrastination is an emotion-regulation problem, we need to look inwards, not outwards.

We don't need windows; we need a mirror.

Our devices are much more useful when we use them to become aware of our emotions rather than give in to them. Instead of escaping on our devices, we can use them to check in with our own minds and untangle the thoughts racing within. It could be as simple as a reminder to meditate, tracking the time we spend on mindless apps, or a journal to write in.

It is not just emotions, though. Using our devices as mirrors means we use them more generally as tools for reflection.

Our devices can help us think more and think clearly. Our total screen time has risen to as high as eleven hours a day on average. It has absorbed all those idle pockets of time when we normally would have thought about hard problems or the future. In Chapter 6, we focus specifically on how to think with computers.

Although these tools for reflection are easily available, we use them rarely or only when we are particularly stressed. However, the best time to fix a leaky roof is when the sun is shining. We need to build regular habits of reflection if we want to break our irrational cycle of escapism.

Chapters 5–6 cover strategies to build such habits.

DON'T SWIM UPSTREAM

How does one quieten their mind?

If we were playing tennis, Gallwey would advise paying attention to the ball. All tennis players are obviously paying attention to the ball. Still, Gallwey asks players to pay attention to the ball like they've never seen one before. To carefully observe how its seams are moving in flight. He also recommends that players say out loud 'Bounce' when the ball bounces and say 'Hit' when their rackets connect with the ball.

Gallwey observed that when his students were absorbed in the rhythmic activity of tracking the ball and saying 'Bounce–Hit', tended to quieten their minds. They become engaged only in the present moment. They are able to play from muscle memory and intuition. Their inner critic quietens down too. They do not have the mental space to get distracted by their self-doubt, judgement or worries about the score. Their better inner game improves their outer game naturally.

The practice of Mindfulness Meditation uses a similar technique. Meditation techniques understand the mind's tendency to wander and do not look upon stray thoughts as a problem. They expect the mind to wander. Every time this happens, they only advise gently bringing back attention to one's breathing. With practice, taking slow, deliberate breaths occupies our complete attention, and our mind quietens.

It is pointless to force the mind to be quiet. Instead, what really makes our mind quiet is *engagement* in an activity. This activity could be as simple as focusing on your breathing or as complex as playing tennis. A quiet mind does not mean that your brain is inactive. In fact, your mind is quiet because your brain is fully occupied by the activity. We are engaged so deeply that we do not have the bandwidth for negative thoughts or distracting mental chatter. Our actions and responses come from a deeper place than our consciousness. Such a state of complete engagement with the task at hand is what Csikszentmihalyi called flow.

Csikszentmihalyi believes that people can experience flow in any part of their lives. To understand the mechanics of flow, Csikszentmihalyi interviewed thousands of people from diverse backgrounds who experienced flow in their work, including Dominican monks, blind nuns and Himalayan climbers, amongst others. In his research, he identified three preconditions for activities that get us into a state of flow.

- The first is to have a clear goal and clarity on how to achieve it.
- Second, there must be immediate feedback to our actions.
- Third, there must be a balance of skill and challenge.

Essentially, taking action towards a well-defined, challenging but achievable goal gets us engaged and into a flow state. You can see these preconditions in action in any video game. Video games are optimized for flow. People who play games regularly will describe the feeling of losing a sense of time and place to the game. Most addictive games give players a goal—either a score or a ranking to maximize. All video games give immediate visual or auditory feedback, including an explicit score, to their players that tell them how they're doing.

As players learn new skills, the challenges presented by the game get increasingly tough. Most games don't give players any rewards for playing, yet people pour hours into them because they induce 'flow'.

Engineering flow makes motivation unnecessary. If you are absorbed in what you are doing, you don't need an explicit reason to do it. At work, we depend on deadlines, commitments or willpower to motivate us to finish our tasks. We do things because we tell ourselves they need to be done. We try to suppress our emotions about the task and force ourselves to work. Motivating oneself to finish a task requires exerting cognitive effort and can be tiring. On the other hand, video games can pull us in even on the days we don't feel like getting much done.

Being in flow means being able to sustain our focus without effort. It is a state of *relaxed* concentration.

Our minds are still highly suggestible. We are usually not aware about how our tongue feels in our mouth, but simply reading this sentence probably shifted your focus onto your tongue. The flow state is both elusive and fragile. Anyone who has experienced it knows it is hard to achieve and easy to lose. For a truly quiet mind, we need to pay attention to *friction*.

In the context of 'flow', friction is anything that requires you to *switch context and apply cognitive effort to another task*. This could be a notification from a messaging app we decided to check or a noisy environment. Besides the usual suspects, it can also be all the stuff that simply gets in our way.

Imagine you are making a presentation for your office. You need to pull up a spreadsheet of the previous quarter's results for a chart. You go looking for the file on your computer. You know you saw it a few days ago, but don't remember what it's called. Soon your focus has moved to the task of finding that spreadsheet. You wander through folders and then eventually land up in your email inbox. While you're there, you end up checking your email. Even when you eventually find the spreadsheet, switching back to the original task is now more challenging since your 'flow' is lost. Your train of thought has been derailed.

Friction is the most overlooked waste of our time. We often blame distractions such as Facebook, email or other notifications for interrupting our work. However, a study has shown that people who have just been interrupted for any reason are *more likely* to check their email or Facebook before getting back to the task they were doing. Thus, on average, workers in the study took anywhere between fifteen and twenty-five minutes to get back to the same state as they were before the interruption. We've all experienced this delay between being interrupted and getting back on task. At twenty minutes per interruption, a dozen such interruptions in a day can mean we waste half our working day *trying* to work rather than working.

The concepts of flow and friction taken together tell us an interesting property of our own attention: Our attention seems to have inertia.

Newton captured the idea of inertia with the first of his three laws of motion. A body at rest or in motion continues to remain at rest or in motion unless acted upon by a force. Something similar happens to our minds. A deeply engaged mind continues to remain engaged on a single topic until context is switched. A distracted mind continues to be distracted until we deeply engage with a new context. Switching between the two states is cognitively hard and costly on our time.

This summarizes the second principle of *bitfulness:* Don't swim upstream.

You wouldn't prepare for exams by taking your books to a nightclub. And although you could, you wouldn't want to drink and dance in a library in daylight. In physical spaces, we understand the obvious idea of a conducive environment. However, we lose sight of the same digitally.

Our technology habits are designed around the hammer model. We expect a superhuman version of ourselves, who cannot be distracted, will show up and execute the task no matter what the environment.

The human brain may have been the inspiration for computers, but it is not a computer itself. We cannot shut down one task and start another seamlessly in our heads as we can on our devices due to attentional inertia. If our environment is distracting, we are spending effort in *trying* to stay focused rather than being completely engaged such that focus is effortless.

Not swimming upstream means that instead of fighting the mind, we learn to quieten it. Chapters 7-10 cover how we can achieve a quiet mind by maximizing flow and minimizing friction.

DEFINE OUR SELVES

No person is an island.

A lot of people feel compelled to check their devices because their workplace, familial obligations or other commitments require them to. The fact that our devices can connect us anytime and anywhere has become as much a curse as it is a gift. We expect everyone to be connected all the time and everywhere. Especially in remote work or when working across time zones, the lines between work and not-at-work start blurring.

It is obvious that this is not healthy. Many workplaces still hold on to the silly idea that longer hours equal sincere, hard workers. In all likelihood, such a culture is burning out one half of employees and creating fear or resentment in the other half who have non-work commitments.

Before the digital era, our routine was divided in both time and space. We left for the office in the mornings in our work clothes. If we were to meet friends, we'd go out in the evenings looking very different. Even if we were to go out with colleagues for a celebration, ties would be loosened, sleeves rolled up and hair let down. These little rituals may seem insignificant, but they acted as signals to our brain. It knew where you are, and therefore *who* you had to be.

People wear many identities. Depending on the context, they are either a parent, a partner, a friend, an employee, a colleague, a boss, a volunteer, a citizen or one of many others. We are so adept at switching our identity throughout the day that we don't even notice we're doing it. Our current internet makes this much harder to do.

Our phones *require* us to switch rapidly between our multiple identities. Whereas once our routine was divided in time and space, a hyperconnected world means that we could be required to act in any capacity at any time. We're not just switching tasks but also identities. One moment you're answering emails to your boss, and the next you are sending memes to your friends. This is how the lines between work and non-work begin to blur.

On the internet, especially on social media, our multiple identities collide because there is context collapse. This means that your posts are on display to multiple audiences simultaneously. You may tell your colleagues that you need to skip the office party to look after your child. Normally, this would be a white lie with no harm and a polite way to refuse. However, it is going to be awkward in the office the next day when someone tags you in a picture from the close friend's party you did go to instead.

As more and more of our life goes online, we are putting a lot of these identities out on the internet. Outside of socially awkward situations, we also have to worry about our privacy. Part of the reason we shifted identities in different contexts was to define how much of ourselves we reveal to others. The Third Crisis is taking away that choice from us in the pursuit of their business model.

Removing the nuances of context and a bounded audience also leads to one of social media's biggest problems—conflict. No matter what our message, or intent behind it, if it reaches an audience that does not share our context, it is very likely to offend or upset someone. Our need for privacy becomes even more critical in this constant conflict. A motivated and skilled actor can cause much financial, reputational or even physical harm with our data.

This brings us to the third principle of *bitfulness*: Define Our Selves.

The skill of moving between our identities and adapting as per context was effortless in the real world. We knew who we were, depending on *where* we were. In the digital world, we have to develop this skill intentionally. Privacy is the act of maintaining this separation of selves, even in the online sphere.

We can't let the internet or social media define who we are, we need to define our selves and limit who has access to each of them. Chapters 11-12 cover strategies to protect your privacy online.

CHOOSING CALMNESS

The mind, as they say, is a wonderful servant but a terrible master.

When we are able to control our attention, quieten our mind and focus on a task, we can achieve great things. However, that is not how we behave by default. Our mind's default response is controlled by our emotions.

This is not a bug but a feature. Our brains help us process the information in our complex environment and past memories to figure out what we should do next. Logical, rational thinking is a useful skill, but survival depends on the speed of our reaction to dangerous situations. We would not survive if we waited for danger to occur before action.

Our emotions offer a shortcut to reasoning. For example, we feel scared when we approach the edge of a cliff in anticipation of a fall. Our body stiffens, we move more carefully and are more alert. From an evolutionary perspective, it would be quite useless if we felt scared only after we fell.

While our emotions are good at predicting what happens if we fall off a cliff, they aren't necessarily well-calibrated to more modern perils. Our emotional predictions are low-fidelity and biased towards survival, making them inaccurate models for our modern, day-to-day tasks.

The Third Crisis further exploits our brain's reward mechanisms. Our time, attention and data drive a large part of the internet economy. We know variable rewards, and other such user-hostile design keeps us addicted. However, even without social media's algorithmic feeds or the flow-inducing immersive worlds of video games, the internet still offers infinite novelty. Novelty itself is highly addictive because of the way it triggers a dopamine release in our heads. It's hard to not feel curious or excited about the unknown and the undiscovered, all from the safety of your phone.

The dread we feel about an assignment is probably not a good prediction of how dangerous it is to us overall. The excitement of a new video posted on social media does not actually correspond to how much satisfaction that video will give us in the long run. Both these emotions are counterproductive for the situation we are in. They drive us to reach for our phones and use them mindlessly instead.

The challenge isn't to stop feeling these emotions. The brain will continue to keep predicting what we should do next, and those predictions will continue to manifest as emotions. The key idea of *bitfulness* is that we become more aware of how our mind works and change the way we use these devices to reflect that understanding.

The real trick is to listen to our emotions and notice when we feel overwhelmed. Are our devices helping us calm down or are they causing the overwhelm? The goal of *bitfulness* is for us to be more self-aware about our emotions during the time we use our devices and change our behaviour so as to be calm. A lot of advice in this book mirrors productivity advice, but the objective isn't to get maximum things done; it is to feel the least stress. Productivity will follow.

In the next eight chapters of this book, we deep dive into each of these three principles. We focus on how to reclaim our time, attention and privacy.

This is, undoubtedly, a hard task. We recommend making these changes one tiny habit at a time. Identify and focus on one behaviour pattern that you want to change. Apply whichever strategies fit you and your problem the best. The best part is that our brains are constantly learning. Do the new behaviour often enough, and you can actually update your brain's defaults, making the new behaviour a habit.

After all, the most daunting opponent is in your own head.

5

HOW TO THINK CLEARLY

THINKING BEFORE DOING

How do you look for keys you've misplaced?

A lot of us, especially if we're in a hurry, tend to start rummaging. We search frantically and in an unfocused manner. We move things around, with no plan in particular. If the keys are in an obvious place, this method works. When they aren't, we tend to spiral.

Not being able to find the keys makes us panic more. Our search becomes even more frantic. We think looking harder means moving more. We jump from one area to the next and often go over the same places again and again. We check the fridge or even under the mattress, just in case.

We already know that the calmer, more effective way to look for our keys is to be systematic. First, try to remember the last moment where you did have the key. Recreate what you did after that in as much detail as possible. Start by looking in the most likely places, and once you've searched an area, do not circle back.

The plan itself is not brilliant, but being aware enough to push back against the panic, and make a plan instead, is a rare trait.

Our instinctive method of thinking is very similar to how we look for the keys. We don't really have a plan. We start rummaging through our mind for all our thoughts about a subject. We often flit from one thought to another. We circle back over the same thoughts. As long as our mind is moving, we think we're making progress.

Our screens exacerbate this tendency. Our devices give us the ability to jump right into things, and we often do so without a plan. Say we're thinking of a larger goal like losing weight. Our minds may start fixating on a minor detail. Usually, something easy and not unpleasant, like which fitness smartwatch we should buy. If we have a screen around, we start looking through reviews and unboxing videos. We will then probably decide to check notifications, scroll through feeds, or get into other such mindless activities before getting back to thinking about our weight.

Technically, we did do something about our goal, but was this really where we were going to find the *key* insight (sorry), or were we just looking in the fridge?

When we focus on a thought, we inherently overestimate its ability to influence us. Daniel Kahneman, the Nobel-prize winning author of *Thinking Fast and Slow*, calls this cognitive bias his 'fortune cookie maxim'. The focusing illusion is pithily surmised by Kahneman as 'Nothing in life is as important as you think it is while you are thinking about it'. Money is the easiest example to understand the focusing illusion. Ask people if being richer would make them happier, and they say yes, because they imagine themselves with better things and fewer problems. Data proves that more money does make people somewhat happier but definitely not as much as they think it will. This difference between fact and reality is what Kahneman calls the 'focusing illusion'.

Thinking is hard. It is even harder to realize when we're thinking irrelevant or unimportant thoughts because of the combined effect of the focusing illusion and our smartphones. Instead of letting these devices be windows we use to escape, we ought to design them as mirrors to reflect on what is on our minds.

Since our current technology is encouraging our tendency to avoid thinking, everyone jumps to the conclusion that we should try to minimize its use. The art of bitfulness frames the problem differently:

Instead of being a tool to avoid thinking, can our technology help us think better?

WRITING IS THINKING

In an *Oral History of Richard Feynman*, a set of interviews recorded and transcribed by historian Charles Weiner, there's an interesting aside that reveals how the great physicist went about his thinking. During the conversation, Feynman has trouble remembering the details of the events Weiner was asking about.

Feynman said, 'If you'll wait a second, I have things by which I can remember. [. . .] So if I look at that thing, I can remember better what I was doing at different times.' The thing that Feynman was describing was his notebooks. The audio breaks here, and the two return after having found the notebooks. Weiner, the historian, sounds very pleased that a 'record' of Feynman's thoughts exists in written form. Feynman responds irritably. He objects to the notebooks being called a 'record'. Later in the same conversation, we get this exchange:

Weiner: Well, the work was done in your head, but the record of it is still here.

Feynman: No, it's not a record, not really, it's working. You have to work on paper, and this is the paper. OK?

What is the relationship of our notes to our thoughts?

Many people believe what Charles Weiner did. Your notes are something you make to record thoughts. It could be your own ideas, facts, appointments, to-do lists but basically a record of things we would rather not forget.

Feynman is suggesting that the notes serve a very different purpose for him. Feynman isn't recording his thoughts for posterity. As he explains, we don't do the thinking in our head, we 'have to work on paper, and this is the paper'. For Feynman, writing *is* thinking.

Not all our thoughts occur to us well-formed. Sometimes, we only have a vague sense of an idea. The process of thinking is the clarifying of this vague sense into concrete knowledge that we can articulate and use. Writing thoughts down helps them develop into something that we can recognize and understand. American author Mary Flannery O'Connor put it in a simpler way—'I write because I don't know what I think until I read what I say.'

Feynman is not the first to have such a collection of thoughts in one place. There are examples dating all the way back to Seneca in the second century AD, and possibly earlier. Many thinkers in history had such notebooks, most famously Leonardo da Vinci. Da Vinci's notes contained ideas that would seem absolutely ridiculous or impossible for the fifteenth century. It also contained measurements of everyday things. But he still wrote those ideas down and even made elaborate drawings of his future inventions. Not all his notes were masterpieces, but the act of writing them down must have helped him think. Why else would he have obsessively written everything down?

Often people resist the idea of writing, because it is 'not for me'. Don't be fooled into thinking that writing is something just writers or academicians or fifteenth-century geniuses do. You are writing your own thoughts for yourself. The quality of the writing doesn't matter as much as the act itself. It is a surprisingly effective way to understand your own thoughts about any part of life. Warren Buffet, another fan of writing to think, once said,

> Some of the things I think I think, I find don't make any sense when I start trying to write them down. You ought to be able to explain why you're taking the job you're taking, why you're making the investment you're making, or whatever it may be. And if it can't stand applying pencil to paper, you'd better think it through some more.

The idea of using an *extended mind* to organize and develop your thoughts is not new. The technology could be as simple as pen and paper. The real difference is in our attitude towards it. We need to be humble about our own ability to think clearly. Both Feynman and Buffett are often portrayed as geniuses of their own respective domains. But even they don't trust their head enough to do all their thinking solely inside it.

Thinking is like any other skill. You get better at it through deliberate practice. Writing is a time-tested, effective way to practise understanding and develop your thoughts. Your extended mind can help make this deliberate practice an effortless habit.

Which is why the first exercise we recommend to think clearly is Bitfulness Meditation.

BITFULNESS MEDITATION

What is Bitfulness Meditation? It is easier to explain in comparison to the Mindfulness Meditation you are probably familiar with.

Both are tools to increase your self-awareness. Mindfulness Meditation teaches you how to ignore all stray thoughts in your mind. Bitfulness Meditation teaches you how to focus on a single train of thought in your extended mind. Mindfulness Meditation is about observing your thoughts without judgement and letting them pass. Bitfulness Meditation is about observing your thoughts without judgement and writing them down.

We recommend following along with this exercise.

1.   Find a comfortable, quiet place

Being disturbed in the middle of this process will not help. So, find a time and place where you are sure you can commit at least fifteen minutes of uninterrupted time.

2.   Create a space on your preferred device to write down your thoughts

This could be a text document on your laptop, the notes app installed by default on your phone, or some other app. You only need to make sure this space is easily accessible and what you write in it remains private. You can even change this later, so just pick one now to get started.

3.   Clear your mind by writing about what's on it

Start a timer for at least five minutes. Now, simply start writing whatever is presently on your mind, in a stream of consciousness style. Make it personal. You can try starting with 'I think . . .' or 'I feel . . .'. Do not try to sound smart or even coherent. Ask yourself questions and then answer them honestly. No one is reading this but you.

Write without any judgement or edits on what you are writing. You do not need to fix typos. You don't even have to stay on one topic. Simply focus on letting your fingers translate your current thoughts into keystrokes till the timer runs out. If you have more to say even after the timer is over, keep going. Many find this part of the exercise is the most beneficial in becoming aware of their emotional states.

4.   Write about what you want to focus on

Once you feel like you've cleared your mind of all thoughts, you can now focus on one task, thought or intention you want to work on. In all likelihood, this worry would have featured in the text you just wrote down in Step 3. Simply start writing about that task. Describe what needs to be done in the same style of writing. If there are any problems or fears, write those down too.

In a fashion similar to Step 3, write without judgement or without correction. If this is hard for you, cover your screen as you write. This way you simply can't read what you've written so far and will be less tempted to make corrections. You may go off topic, and your mind may begin to wander. Whenever you sense that you have gone too far astray, pause. Simply scan a few lines up, and pick up from where you left off.

You can use a timer to decide when to stop or simply write till you feel clarity of thought.

5.   Step back and reflect on what you just wrote

Now that all your worries and doubts are out of your head, you should be feeling a slight sense of calm. Depending on how much you wrote, you must be feeling either a slight or great increase in your sense of control. You're no longer in the grip of the 'focussing illusion'. Read through what you've written and without editing or deleting, summarize for yourself what your thoughts are telling you to do.

Hopefully, the next immediate action for you to take is clear, and so is your motivation to do it.

Why does this work?

This exercise works because it is nothing but a form of journaling. If you tried it, you might have felt some clarity. If you didn't, you're probably skeptical that writing your thoughts for a few minutes is going to make a dent to the big problems in your life.

A lot of scientists were skeptical too so they put it to the test. Psychologists and neuroscientists alike have found that journaling correlates with tremendous health benefits, even if they are unable to ascertain why. Journaling reduces stress, helps you cope with anxiety, increases positive mood, reduces symptoms of depression, improves interpersonal relationships and even increases your 'working memory'. Studies have shown that gratitude journals, where people record a list of things that they are grateful for, even when recorded only once a week, boost happiness.

Anyone who journals will readily tell you its mental health benefits. Where it starts to get eye-popping is when you see reports of expressive journaling being the difference that leads to lower blood pressure, significantly better quantity and quality of sleep, increased T-Cell count and even faster healing of wounds. The most probable explanation is that journaling lets you identify your own stress and helps deal with it better, leading to health benefits. Simply writing down what's bothering you converts it from an abstract, all-consuming worry into something much more contained and manageable.

Every time you start to feel stuck, overwhelmed or stressed, your head is probably full of thoughts that you haven't untangled yet. The brain has a *working memory* that works similarly to that of a computer's RAM. Whatever we're thinking about needs to be held in the working memory, and it has a limited capacity. Any form of journaling empties your working memory, making more room to think. Doing it digitally, like in Bitfulness Meditation, helps create a habit of being self-aware while being in front of a screen. It becomes a ritual that helps you ease into a state of relaxed concentration. It also creates a record of those thoughts, so that you can later analyse what's happening in your own head to unstick yourself.

Often we try to plan our next move by thinking hard. We have a jumble of ideas and problems, and we think of an action but also think of a downside to that action. We think of other things we should be doing and other things causing us worry. All of these interweaving thoughts send us into analysis paralysis. We try to 'think harder', but we're just doing more of the same incoherent mess.

However, writing *is* thinking. You're not really planning unless you're writing your plan down. To-do lists or business plans force us to crystallize our thoughts into actions *before* we write them down. Like O'Connor and Buffet, we too won't know what our thoughts are trying to tell us till we write them down so that we can read them. By building the habit of Bitfulness Meditation and writing freely, we think about structure *after* we've emptied our mind of all our thoughts. Thus, letting us think clearly about what we need to do.

We can only guess why this practice works, but we can assure you that it does.

The next time you're feeling overwhelmed or stuck, repeat this exercise. You can repeat it as often as you need, as many times a day as you want. But to really benefit from writing as thinking, we need to build this practice into a *system*.

HOW TO BE MORE SELF-AWARE

Pausing to think clearly helps us do more than just locate our keys.

Often, our first thoughts are not our best ones. Taking some time to be patient and deliberate with our thinking would help in doing most things. However, we know thinking is hard. Thinking takes time and effort. It also doesn't give the impression of doing much. Whereas, taking decisive action based on our first thought *feels* like progress.

Time spent thinking does not take more time; it frees it up. The point of thinking isn't always to generate brilliant ideas. Thinking deliberately helps us see all the ways in which we take useless action. Taking time to think helps us prioritize and plan so that we need to take *less* action for the same results, and feel much calmer while doing so.

To build a consistent habit of thinking clearly requires making the *process* of thinking significantly easier. To do this, we believe that everyone needs an explicit *working memory*. That is, we want a central place where everything we want to think about is written. From our working memory, the process of clarifying, organizing, and processing our thoughts can begin.

This is the simplest 'hack' that you can implement to break the toxic relationship with your screen. Currently, every time you feel overwhelmed, anxious or unmotivated, you use your screen as a window to escape. With a working memory, you gain the ability to use it as a mirror, to reflect on what's really going on in your head. Its effectiveness is determined by how *consistently* you use it to think.

You can use the notes app you chose in the Bitfulness Meditation, or something else, to be your *working memory*. There are now many types of note-taking apps and word editors, all of which have fanbases that claim they'll help you build 'a second brain'. Pick any one, since the most value comes from collecting all your thoughts in the same place, rather than any other feature. What really matters is accessibility: having the ability to record and retrieve your thoughts easily, wherever you are, online or offline.

Even if you already write to think, collecting your thoughts in one place has many advantages. The obvious advantage is that you can much easily find things you had forgotten or misremembered. But once you build a consistent habit of thinking by writing, it lets you see your own thinking evolve with time. This is what Feynman did in his notebooks.

When Weiner first read Feynman's notes, he thought they were a record because of the way they were written. On the audio, he remarks that Feynman wrote them,

> almost in a first-person diary form asking yourself questions and then setting out an agenda for work, indicating you spoke to so-and-so today and you got this idea and then you want to pose yourself a certain agenda and then tackling it. Each page is dated. Some pages have a later date on them because you have gone back to them and said, well, this problem didn't work out, or it was solved in terms of the work done on 5 June 1968, or incorporated into that. And so this represents the record of the day-to-day work.

The way Weiner describes it, Feynman seemed to be mapping his thoughts to work with them, rather than put down a record. The text wasn't static, but something that changed as his mind did.

Even in our digital world, Feynman's notebooks have a lot to teach abut how to build our *working memory*.

Feynman is also known to have said, 'If you can't explain something in simple terms, you don't understand it'. The notebooks tell us that Feynman didn't wait to find some novice to explain physics to. He used his working memory to have a conversation with his own thoughts. He clarified his thoughts by explaining them to *himself,* which is what probably made him such a great explainer. He put a date on each page and then started writing what he thought he should be doing, whom he spoke to, and even questions he'd answer months later.

We recommend doing the same thing in your 'working memory'. Make sure there's a new page or section for each date, and then note everything worth noting that day on that page. You can plan your day. Ask yourself questions in first-person form, and write down your own answers without judgement. If you do the Bitfulness Meditation exercise, that could also be written here. Essentially, you can capture any information that you want, as long as you're capturing it all in one place. Having determined an explicit place to do all your thinking reduces the friction that comes from the question of 'where do I store this?'.

The rule to follow is simple—Everything you think today goes on today's page in your working memory.

Some of these thoughts will lead to actions. A lot of thoughts will simply collect in your working memory, ready to be retrieved when you next need them. We will cover how to process these in a later chapter. If you're just beginning, worry more about consistently capturing your thoughts than organizing them. Habits are built by repetition.

Think of the working memory as a framework for daily reflection rather than just a collection of notes. You can capture progress on a habit you're trying to build by noting down if you did or did not do it that day. You can make journal entries to track your mood as well. You could also store external information you came across that you find interesting or useful as Da Vinci did. It could be ideas, quotes, jokes, recipes or stories too. All the half-thought thoughts that you plan on thinking more about later can go here too.

There are advantages to being able to record things quickly and think about them later. For example, you can understand how consistent you've been with your habits by looking back over the data. There's also the case of losing information because you don't use it in time. Often people recommend a book, podcast, movie, article or artist to us just when we don't have the time. You can write this down in your working memory, including details on who recommended what. Whenever you do have the time to read or watch something, you can browse through your list of recommendations, rather than surfing the internet. It might even prompt you to send the person who recommended it a thoughtful thank you.

If you already do some version of note-taking, you may have observed a problem. When your notes become numerous, it is hard to find something if you only vaguely recollect what to search for. Search fails because it requires you to remember exactly what you wrote. The easiest way around this problem is to 'Save by Context'. In practice, saving by context means to tag extensively and generously while making notes. In your notes, you can just add #idea, #quotes, #recommendation, #habit or other such tags to group related ideas. There's very little penalty to over-tagging, and there is no such thing as too many tags. The tags and links help create multiple paths to land at the same chunk of knowledge. Since you save these notes by date anyway, they are already associated with the context of other things on that day.

If you save by context sincerely, you are able to not only retrieve ideas you had weeks or years ago but also retrace your steps and see what else you were up to when you had that idea.

Over time, your working memory will become the starting point for all your future work. It contains all the hard-earned knowledge and wisdom you've learnt over the years. By writing down your own thoughts in one place, you ensure that you don't have to think the same thought twice. You can make reusable lego blocks of knowledge that you can use to construct more advanced and original thoughts.

USING YOUR WORKING MEMORY AS A PLATFORM FOR REFLECTION

Like we said, the working memory is a platform for reflection. It really is a wonderful tool that can help us excel at anything we're trying to be more thoughtful about.

Sharad Sharma of iSPIRT uses his technology to be more thoughtful in conversations. One of the remarkable things about

Sharad is how he can recall details of past conversations you have had with him. If you ask him for advice, he often recalls, in merry detail, conversations he has had with others who have been in a similar bind as you. You may have mentioned a trivial fact to Sharad about your family or a worry about a project. Sharad makes it a point to ask about it in the next conversation, even if the next conversation is months later.

Sharad says that his memory is actually terrible, he simply follows a system inspired by Azim Premji. In the summer of 2004 in Bangalore, Sharad had a fleeting moment of conversation with Premji at an event. Sharad invited Premji, who was then India's richest man, to give a speech at his company in Pune. Premji promised that whenever he was in Pune next, he would get in touch. Sharad assumed this was a busy man politely declining another request for his time.

Sharad was surprised when in January of 2005, Premji's office got in touch. Premji was coming to Pune and had asked his office to arrange a talk at Sharad's company if Sharad was still willing. Sharad says he had nearly forgotten that brief exchange and was mind-blown that Premji remembered. When the two finally met, Sharad asked Premji how he had managed to follow up after all that while.

Premji told him that he aspired to be a man of his word, so he made it a point to deliver on all his promises, whether small or big. Premji showed Sharad a set of 5×7 index cards he carried, on which he wrote down all promises he made that day. He later filed them in a way that made them easy to recall when he needed them. This is how he remembered a quick promise made in a corridor, more than six months later. Not superhuman memory, merely a system of storing information and retrieving it as needed.

Five years later, Sharad quit his job and started iSPIRIT to help Indian start-ups build world-class technology products out of India. In his new role as an ecosystem builder, he says his success was making sure others succeeded. He wanted to help Indian entrepreneurs reach their personal definition of success. He had dozens of conversations with entrepreneurs every week. He wanted to make sure he was helpful to each of them on their own personal journey.

He soon realized that he couldn't help them in just one conversation. Nor could he do it if he had forgotten their definition of success by the next time he met them. So, inspired by Premji, he created his own working memory system.

Here's how Sharad's system works. Whenever he has a few quick minutes, he uses a note-taking software to record the highlights of every conversation he has had with people throughout the day, often in the car ride right after a meeting. He has these organized by the name of the individual to see the thread of conversation. He says that recording isn't that hard once the habit kicks in. Over time you learn to calibrate what's worth recording and what's not. One persists when one sees the value in it.

We often think of our digital devices as places where we go to do digital work or where we go for entertainment. When we think of our devices as extended minds, we can use them to help change how we think and behave in the real world. We would all like to be as dependable as Premji or as thoughtful as Sharad. What this story tells us is that these are not innate personality traits; we can build a system that helps us become so.

You could use a working memory for cultivating any good habit or getting rid of a bad one. You could use it to be more thoughtful in our relationships or at work. These are all things that a working memory helps you *do*.

The more important question in designing your working memory is what do you want it to help you *become*?

LONG-TERM MEMORY

STORAGE AND SEARCH

The analogy between computer and human memory is useful in our quest on how to think better.

Memory serves two purposes in computers and humans. We already spoke about RAM or working memory. The other kind of memory is what goes on your hard disks—basically, a space for long-term storage and retrieval.

Computers are excellent at long-term storage, and humans are prone to forgetting. Theoretically, we could just store everything we need to remember on our devices. But the problem is one of retrieval.

Where should I keep this file, so that future-me can retrieve it easily? Where should I write down this information so that I won't be hunting for it when I need it? Where do I save this task so that I know it will be done in the future?

You may be thinking that computers have search. There is one wrinkle. Computers search by comparison. Whereas, our memories work by association. The most unique thing you may remember about a PDF you're trying to find is that your friend recommended it to you. If one can only remember a small fragment of that document's contents, search will be useless. Also, search results become noisier the more you store.

Is there a way to organize our long-term storage that can guarantee we will find the exact files we need when we need them?

Well, the simple answer is—No. The fundamental problem is that the only person who can answer if an organizing system is useful is future-you. We do not have a way of divining what our future self will be searching for. Organizing systems often fail because of this fundamental unknowability. We overinvest in creating structure, but that structure turns out to be useless anyway.

At the same time, clutter on our devices can feel stifling and overwhelm us. We've all wasted time looking for that important file. Worse, we start looking for the file, only to end up working on something else entirely. Organizing often becomes an activity done for its own sake, to create a false sense of order and peace.

Our take is that the system that is easiest to maintain is the system that works. We need some organization, but don't want to invest too much time in doing it. If your system requires significant upkeep, it is not a good system. Since the best organizational structure is fundamentally unknowable, it might be useful then to leave most of the task to our future self. Instead of investing heavily in organizing, we will do the *least possible required*. While you can't be sure what the future-you will be looking for, we can make sure the future-you is looking for a needle in a drawer, not in a haystack. Anything more would be premature optimization.

If you already have such a system in place, skip this section. But if you don't, we can tell you what works for us.

THE TOP-LEVEL HIERARCHY

We believe that you only need to have three top-level folders—Desktop, Downloads and Documents—on any computer or even mobile. These correspond to files that you need immediately, temporarily, and in the long run, respectively.

The Desktop is for files that you are currently working on. It acts as an inbox for files that need your attention soon. You should strive to have absolutely no files on your Desktop except those currently required or in a queue to process. Once completed, the file can either move to long-term storage in Documents or be deleted if unnecessary.

The Downloads folder is for temporary storage. Let's say you download a PDF report on COVID-19 cases in your area that day. You do not need this information again. Instead of filing it, you can safely leave it in your downloads. Your downloads folder should always be in a state where even if all files in it are suddenly deleted, you will not miss any of them. Your browser, email application and all others should download files to this folder by default. If there is a file that you may need longer than an instant, consciously move it to Desktop or file it in Documents.

The Documents folder is your long-term storage. This is where everything that matters to you lives. This is where you will need to go when you're trying to search for a file you have worked on previously. You may also need to store receipts, tax records, health records and other such minutiae.

If you strictly keep data only in these three folders and nowhere else, you solve one of the most important problems with long-term data—backups. We recommend setting up a cloud storage account to automatically backup your Desktop and Documents folders to the cloud. The advantage of this is simply peace of mind. Even if you lose your devices at any point of time, your most important files will always be safe and accessible.

The problem of organizing knowledge amongst many scientists at CERN is why Tim Berners-Lee invented the World Wide Web in the first place. Instead of hierarchies, the hypertext markup language (HTML) championed the use of links. Multiple branches of associative links emanating from every document make up the 'web' of the world wide web. Links reduce the friction in following your train of thought to the document or information you really need. Links can be referenced easily in other documents, notes and emails so that the file is available in context.

Other than backup, links are the other advantage to cloud storage. Most cloud storage providers will provide a unique link, i.e., URL, for every file we upload. This link remains consistent even if we change the folder in which it is placed or change the filename. This makes links even more robust, especially for sharing files and folders with others who may have their own way of organizing their files. You can simply add this link to your working memory with relevant hashtags to remember the context. This makes finding the file even easier since it associates the file with all sorts of context for that day.

If you only organize into three folders, back up to the cloud and save links in your working memory, you have a fairly robust system. You should just be okay with the mess inside these three folders. By simply separating the current and the important from the temporary, you will solve a lot of your problems. However, if you can't or don't want to trust online cloud storage services, in the next section, we dive deeper into organizing your Documents folder.

ORGANIZING YOUR DOCUMENTS

Once you have all your long-term files in your Documents folder, they can still become quite a mess if not attended to. Here's a simple algorithm to organize them.

- Create a folder for every new project you begin
- Put as much context as you can in the *name* of the folder.
- Store everything related to the project in that folder and nowhere else.
- Whenever you need a file, search for the folder and look in it for your file.

This sounds very simple, and it really is!

First, a project is a specific outcome that you are trying to drive by a particular date. For example, suppose you are collaborating with

Rahul to publish an annual report for your startup by December of 2021. In that case, the folder name could be '2021-12 Startup Annual Report with Rahul'. If you remember even some of those details, then you should be able to locate the folder.

Trying multi-level hierarchies, or splitting files by categories such as home and personal, is not really necessary if you follow this method. If you really have more context that you want to include, add it to the folder's name, rather than hiding that folder inside another.

The advantage of putting the date and month upfront consistently is that you can create a timeline of your projects inside your Documents folder by sorting. Having this timeline in a flat structure instead of in hierarchies may also reveal additional clues from context, which will help your brain with recall. For example, you may not remember the exact name of a project. Still, you remember it was happening around the same time as when you were planning a community fundraiser. You can search for the fundraiser instead. Then one of the project folders just above and below may be the one you are looking for.

Some categories, such as health records or family photos, are timeless. You may want to group these together. We recommend using your birth date as the project date for these. This way, these folders will collect either at the bottom (or top) of your documents folder. Your most recent projects will always collect at the top (or bottom) of the documents folder. This makes life simpler, without having to really organize too much. Such a system adapts to your context, without having to put in the effort.

If the records inside these folders get really numerous, split them into two projects to make the containers small again. The number of project folders should not concern you, just as the number of webpages on the internet doesn't. The idea is to rely on search to narrow down, not go through the list of folders one by one.

If you are just starting on this method and have a mess of files on your computer, just put them all together in one new folder with today's date and call the project 'Archive'. Do not attempt to organize that folder now or in the future, unless the need really arises. We access our archives a lot less often than we think.

If you find yourself going back into the archives for specific files, pull those files out of archives and put them in an appropriately named folder.

This is a battle-tested method. Nandan has been organizing his projects this way for nearly twenty-five years. In 2019, when the legendary American economist Paul Volcker passed away, Nandan wanted to post a tribute to him. His fondest memory was a fishing trip he had organized for Volcker, an avid fisher, near Bangalore. He quickly retrieved from his folder system a picture that was then *twelve years old*. Because he had saved it in a folder called 2007-02 Volcker India Visit.

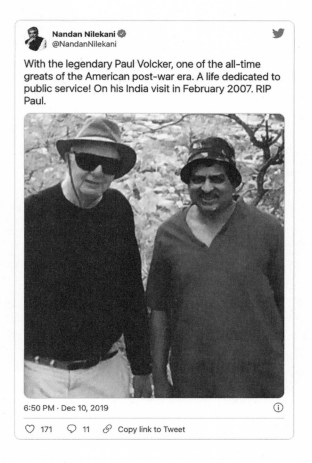

Nandan Nilekani ✓
@NandanNilekani

With the legendary Paul Volcker, one of the all-time greats of the American post-war era. A life dedicated to public service! On his India visit in February 2007. RIP Paul.

6:50 PM · Dec 10, 2019

♡ 171   ♡ 11   🔗 Copy link to Tweet

CLEAR YOUR MIND

None of the strategies we suggested are set in stone. There are many software tools and knowledge frameworks on how to journal and how to organize your data. Pick whatever works for you. If it isn't working, try something else. If you're just getting started, focus more on creating a habit of capturing your thoughts, notes and files consistently. Once you are able to do that consistently, you can optimize further.

The only thing that matters is that you instinctively know where to save something so that it is out of your head, but not lost.

Remember, thinking is hard, and there is no need to make finding your own data harder than it needs to be. Together, your working memory and long-term storage offer a way to offload a large part of your thinking and remembering onto your extended mind. This helps bring clarity in your thoughts.

However, thinking clearly alone is not going to solve our problems, if we're not thinking about the right things. The next chapter talks about how our devices can help us not just think better but also focus on what's important.

6

WHAT TO THINK ABOUT

LOSING TIME

Have you experienced a long, busy day of much activity only to realize that you didn't even start what you set out to finish?

In 2016, Francesca Gino, a professor at Harvard Business School, and her colleagues analysed the data from 43,000 patient encounters at Emergency Departments of hospitals. They found that when the number of patients arriving increases, the Emergency Department (ED) doctors start dealing with 'easy' patients first.

It is not an unreasonable system. Since more patients were coming in, more patients needed to get out. The easy patients could be treated faster. However, easy patients usually corresponded to less sick patients. They could probably have waited without their condition deteriorating much. The ones who ended up waiting were the serious patients, for whom the wait could make things worse. Moreover, when the serious patients did get their turn, doctors were likely to be more tired and less effective because of all the patients they had to treat before.

Behavioural scientists call this tendency to tackle easy things first 'completion bias'.

Completing a task gives us an immediate psychological reward. The quick win can even help up our self-confidence and motivation for the next task. The problem starts when this motivational trick turns into a toxic pattern. Like the ED doctors faced with a surge of patients, we get into a habit of only doing the easy things while the hard things get sicker.

Completion bias is why even when we don't waste time on distractions, it often still feels like time slipped through our fingers. We complete easier, smaller tasks and it makes us feel productive in the short-run. But over the long run, doing small tasks doesn't feel like fulfilling progress.

Most of us are likely to have some system of calendars and to-do lists, but success in sticking to these varies. Often the problem with these is that they are designed for a narrow definition of productivity— i.e., getting the maximum number of things done.

In the internet age, productivity is not a quantity problem, but a quality problem. Doing things has become easier—you can get products delivered straight to your house, you can hire professionals online, you can automate bill payments, you can set up meetings on video and you can look up any information at any time.

The progress goes both ways, though. It is now much easier for people to reach us via email, text or call and add to our list of things to do. Because of all that choice and incoming information, it is easy to get overwhelmed. Doing things has become easier, but doing the *right* things has become much harder.

It doesn't have to be this way. Your extended mind can not only help you think *better* but can also help you decide *what* you should be thinking about. This chapter is about how to focus your attention on the things that truly matter.

If you already have a system for picking the right things to do, you can safely skip ahead to the next chapter (Chapter 7) where we cover strategies for sticking to the task. If not, let us see how we can align our attention with our intentions.

PRESENT SELF VS FUTURE SELF

The reason we find it difficult to do the *right* things is because we think of our future selves in the same way in which we think of strangers.

Imagine yourself at your birthday party, twenty years from now. Most people would imagine themselves in third person, looking at their older selves from outside, as if watching a movie. Whereas, when you think of more present experiences, like your next birthday, you probably imagine yourself in first person, blowing out the candles on your cake.

We don't just imagine our future selves as strangers; we behave as if they are strangers too. In a study called 'Doing Unto Future Selves As You Would Do Unto Others: Psychological Distance and Decision Making', students at a university were asked how much time they could dedicate to tutoring weaker students. The researchers asked students to predict how much time they could dedicate in the current and next semester, as well as how much time they believed their friends could volunteer for the same task. They were cautious with their own time in the current semester but believed that their friends and future selves would have much more time than their current self.

Social psychologist Hal Hershfield of the UCLA Anderson School of Management went one step further and actually measured how people thought about their future selves under an MRI machine. His studies showed that when we think of our future selves, the same regions of the brain get activated as when we think about strangers. Building on his research, he showed retirement savers a picture of themselves aged algorithmically by thirty years. Those who saw the pictures saved roughly 40 per cent more than those who weren't shown the picture.

Our brains are deeply wired to prefer short-term pleasure, even when it comes at long-term costs to ourselves. Whether it is eating a slice of cake, or procrastinating that assignment, we prioritize the needs and wants of our present self. We treat our future selves as though they will somehow have more clarity, willpower, determination or strength than our present selves. We expect them to work like machines and not have the same human foibles that we have currently. We just need to look at our past record to see that this is untrue.

Instead of sabotaging our future selves, we need to learn to work together.

We all know what we want from our future selves. We want to be more successful at work, become healthier, spend more time with loved ones or finish a passion project. Even though we know what we want, our plan on how to get it is often vague.

Think about which of these is more effective—'I will lose 10 kilos' versus 'I will do ten squats before I sit at my desk'. An imprecise intention leads to insufficient motivation. Without a predetermined plan with clear intentions, we get overwhelmed by the infinite choice the internet offers us. Our day begins to drift away from us. As the day progresses, our attention moves further and further away from our already vague intentions.

Planning helps, but only up to a point. The more detailed your plan, the less room it has for disruptions. Once your day begins to veer off course, every time you finish a task, you have to make a fresh decision— 'What should I be doing now?' You are likely to start completing unimportant tasks or, worse, fall into a distraction rabbit hole.

In the best-selling *Inner Game of Tennis*, Timothy Gallwey diagnoses correctly that most people do not need coaching on technique. The problem is 'not that I don't know what to do, it's that I don't do what I know!'. According to Gallwey, sportsmen trying to improve are hampered less by their lack of knowledge and more by the voices of self-criticism in their own head. They are listening to the internalized words of others telling them how they are wrong and what they should fix. What Gallwey advises is to quieten the mind. Instead of paying attention to the criticism, he advises paying attention to the ball instead. He encourages them to be fully immersed in the game by observing the ball and saying 'Bounce' and 'Hit'. He offers no further instructions and simply lets players focus on their game. Usually, he says, people learn to fix their own problems without further coaching.

If you feel like you aren't using your time to the fullest, you probably already know what to do, but doing it is hard. Criticizing yourself for being too busy, procrastinating too much or wasting too much time is unlikely to help. Like all the tennis players Gallwey has coached, what we need isn't a more advanced technique, but rather a return to the basics. Before reacting emotionally to it, we need to truly observe where our time is going. We need a simple way to become mindful of where our time *is* going, versus where it is *supposed to be* going.

The goal of this part of the book is to develop such an anchor for our time. A simple structure to keep us moored to our intentions, but with enough slack that we can deal with the natural ebb and flow of the day. We also need to cultivate awareness to notice when we're drifting away from the plan. Doing the right things with our time comes down to mastering two related skills, each of which can be done more mindfully with the help of our devices.

1. Making Time
2. Using Time

MAKING TIME

SHOW ME YOUR CALENDAR, AND I'LL TELL YOU YOUR PRIORITIES

If time is money, why do so many people pinch pennies but waste away hours?

Here's a simple exercise to get you thinking about how your time aligns with your intentions. In your working memory page for today, create a list of your most important priorities—What are the top five goals in your life that you want to give time to? Now, evaluate your calendar from the last week and write down how much time you actually gave to these priorities. It is important to do this in writing, so that you can hold yourself accountable. Be honest, and write zero if it is zero.

The time and money equivalence is more than just a cliché. Your time is the most valuable asset in the world. Every objective that you want from your life needs time, and there's only so much you can give. Unlike money, even if someone else has time to spare, you cannot borrow or steal it from them. You may be able to delegate some work, but no one else can spend time with your family on your behalf, which means that *your* time should be focused on *your* biggest priorities.

You need to realize that ultimate control over how you spend your time resides only with you. All of us have obligations, but even if you only have an hour to yourself every day, you decide how you spend that hour. You decide how you're going to get the maximum out of it. People say they can't find the time to work on their goals. However, time is something you *make*, not find.

If your biggest priorities do not have space on your schedule, then you're not busy, you're just procrastinating.

Some people feel the same helplessness about their money. They think they don't have enough to save for the future. The most important advice financial advisors give clients is to change the way they think about savings. Usually, people think that their Savings = Income – Expenses. Financial advisors teach us that this equation is actually Expenses = Income – Savings.

PAY YOURSELF FIRST.

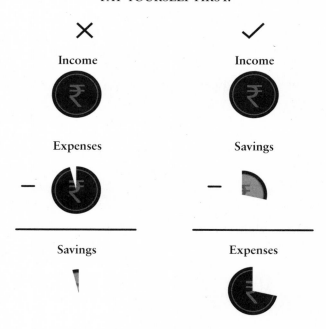

- Set aside savings first, not your expenses.
- This is non-negotiable, automate it.
- Whatever money remains, can be spent guilt-free.

If we spend what we want and save the rest, we will always spend more and save less. A better way is to treat our savings like rent, i.e., as our first and most important expense that we cannot skip. When you get paid, first set aside the amount you want to save to meet your goals. Then pay for all critical expenses such as rent, food and utilities. What is leftover can be spent in any which way you desire. When we budget money, we can save enough as well as enjoy spending guilt-free. Building the habit of saving is extremely valuable, even if we save a very small amount.

We want to budget our time in a similar way.

Rather than picking the easy things, we want to first spend time on our most important priorities. Instead of responding to emails or clearing out your to-do list, look at your priorities and ask—'What's the most important thing I can do today to make progress towards my goals?' Even if you do just one thing in a day, as long as it is a step towards your goal, it is a day well spent. You can spend the rest of the day doing whatever you feel like, and it would be a bonus if you got any additional work done.

YOUR TIME IS MONEY, SPEND IT ON YOURSELF FIRST.

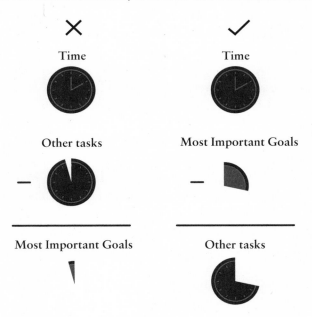

- Do the important tasks first, not last.
- Block this time on your calendar.
- Whatever time remains, can be spent guilt-free.

The easiest way to implement this strategy is a method called time blocking.

MAKE TIME BY BLOCKING TIME

Time blocking is a stupidly simple method to make time for your goals.

Instead of hoping to get to work on something important at some time today, you make a commitment to do it at a specific time. The idea is as simple as it sounds, but it can be highly effective in practice. The easiest way to find out is to try it yourself.

In your calendar, block a chunk of time for your most important work. You don't need to know currently what that work is. All you need to commit to is that during this time, you will only be doing your most important work and nothing else. Do not schedule any other event or call in this period.

If possible, make this a ritual. Block the same time every day for your most important work. Preferably, this time is early in the morning so that other events don't get a chance to disrupt your day before you get to it. Sit in the same spot, grab your favourite beverage, put your phone away, and let everyone know you're not to be disturbed. The more consistent you are, the easier it will be for your mind to settle in and focus.

Time blocking helps make time for important tasks but can also be a way to limit time for unimportant tasks. You can make thirty-minute blocks for checking email or checking social media, and commit to yourself that you will only do these activities within that time block.

Often, when we're trying to change our own behaviour, we bite off more than we can chew. Don't try to micromanage your whole day. We recommend you start by creating one block only for your most important task and focus on meeting that commitment each day. Only when you feel confident in your ability to stick to your first block of time, then add another. Behaviour change is more effective when we treat it as a muscle to be built with repetition.

People who use time blocks further benefit from dividing their blocks by context rather than content. Even if you have multiple projects going on, it might be useful to block your mornings for deep work, and your afternoons for meetings. This helps minimize context switching, which can quickly drain your time. You can schedule creatively demanding work when you are most creative and answer emails when you are not. A simple way to enforce this time block is through automated calendar assistants. [See the Appendix for a list of apps.] These allow you to set up time blocks for meetings and allow anyone to book an open slot directly via a link.

Time blocking is remarkably simple but effective. But, it won't save our day unless we throw away our to-do list.

THROW AWAY YOUR TO-DO LIST

The most common contract between our present selves and our future selves is the to-do list.

Our present selves write down things that we expect our future selves will do. Our future selves do the best they can, but the list never seems to end. It is obvious why the list only grows—it is much easier to write down a task in our to-do list than it is to clear things out of it. When we can't decide what to do about a task, we simply write it down in our to-do list and make it our future-self's problem. These overhanging, unimportant tasks then compete for attention with the important ones. Every time we look at the list, we have to make a decision on 'What should I be doing now?' Like the ED doctors, we tend to pick the easy to-dos first. This leaves us with no time for the harder tasks. We write them down on our to-do lists instead, and the pattern of bad decisions perpetuates.

There's a simple solution to this problem—throw away your to-do lists.

A task without the time to do it is a wish, not a to-do. These wishes only weigh us down. When we don't have a to-do list, we're forced to make decisions now rather than leave both planning and doing to our future self. How does one get things done without a to-do list?

First, if the task is easy enough to do immediately, do it. Don't keep things pending that don't need to be. If you need to send an email after a meeting or share your notes, do it immediately. Leave a gap between your appointments so that you can use it to 'wrap-up' your previous session. Since the context is still fresh, doing this task takes less time now than it would if you did it later. Getting a sense of completion right then and there will help you concentrate fully on your next task. Moreover, tasks that could be done immediately don't become baggage for later.

If a task can't be done immediately, think about the next actionable step. The more clear, specific and atomic you make the next step, the less time your future self has to spend in figuring out the task.

Finally, put this actionable next step into your calendar.

In a 2001 paper, British researchers showed that a single intervention helped jump up the number of people exercising at least once a week. There was a control group and two treatment groups. When the results came, in 35 per cent of the people in the control group had exercised once a week. However, 38 per cent of the people in treatment group A and a whopping 91 per cent in the treatment group B exercised. What was the difference?

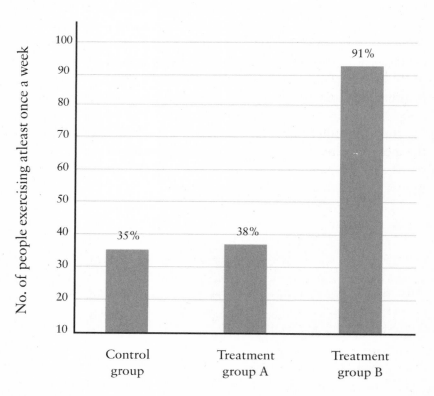

Treatment Group A participants were told the benefits of exercise. However, Treatment Group B had to write down their intentions explicitly. Each member of the group had to write down 'During the next week, I will partake in at least 20 minutes of vigorous exercise on [DAY] at [TIME] in [PLACE].'

Deciding the time and place for when you're going to do an action automatically increases the chances of you doing it. Putting this intention on your calendar helps turn this insight into a habit. If you use time blocking, this becomes significantly easier to do, since you will have your day roughly divided into blocks of focus already.

Using your calendar as your to-do list acts as the missing link between your time and your workload. Your calendar becomes the one place where you have all the information about what you need to do next. You are now able to think about using your time more meaningfully since it lists out all the promises you've already made.

Initially, putting tasks on your calendar will seem more cumbersome than making a simple to-do list, but the friction is the point. It forces you to realistically consider how much time you have. If you don't think about the time you genuinely have, you might overpromise and underdeliver.

If you still think you don't have time, you probably don't know the most effective productivity trick known to mankind.

USING TIME

THE MOST EFFECTIVE PRODUCTIVITY
TRICK KNOWN TO MANKIND

We make much more prudent decisions with our money than we do with our time.

You wouldn't buy a Mercedes if you could only afford a Maruti. Yet we sign up for tasks and projects, whether work or personal, that require more of our time than we can afford. Moreover, the guilt of those unfinished projects weighs on us, adding to our stress, clouding our mind.

The single biggest productivity trick known to mankind is saying 'no'.

We say yes to projects because we see them as exciting or interesting. We don't think about whether they are exciting *enough* for the time they will require. Every 'yes' is an investment of our time. Just like with money, if the investment isn't generating sufficient returns we should get out, and not sink more money (or time) on a bad decision.

Ultimately, time is zero-sum. If you've signed up for more work at the office, you are probably spending less time with family or on your hobbies. Unlike your bank balance, you don't see your time balance deplete when you overspend your time on something you can't afford. This lack of feedback can be actively harmful.

One helpful tool in deciding when to say 'no' is a time budget.

On a new page in your working memory, create your time budget. Out of the twenty-four hours in a day, we need at least seven or more hours for sleep. We need another two to four hours for exercise, meals, hygiene and other daily chores around the house. We should be making the time to spend with friends and family too. Out of the 168 hours we have every week, just these would take away roughly half or more of our time. We still need to subtract the unavoidable things like meetings we can't skip, time spent on commuting and social or familial obligations. The idea is to not sweat the details but to just make an estimate.

Your budget need not be precise down to the last minute. It is only a tool to help us make better decisions about what we can and cannot commit to. Think of it like the fuel gauge on our car. It won't tell us exactly how many litres of fuel we have, but over time, we get better at deciding if we have enough to make the trip or not.

In any given week, on average, you may have maybe thirty hours to spend on your goals—let's call these your time balance. Your personal number may be a bit higher if you have fewer obligations. Your time balance is the number of hours that are actually available to you to split among your work, your hobbies and any leisure time.

Now 'invest' your time balance towards things that matter to you. Use the priorities you wrote down in the previous exercise. Be careful to not use up all of your time balance, though. You should ideally also have spare time for unplanned exigencies, serendipity or just being idle.

If it looks like you aren't able to make enough time to actually do justice to one or more of your goals, the problem isn't that you're not productive. The problem is that you're trying to do too much. You have to drop something or you risk doing everything poorly. You also have to refuse any additional projects till your time budget goes up again. Calculating your time budget every few weeks or after the start and end of projects will help you make better decisions about your commitments.

People feel uncomfortable saying no because they are concerned they will come across as snobbish. In our experience, this is untrue. People appreciate clear, rapid and genuine answers irrespective of whether that answer is favourable to them or not. Going from a gut-based system to a framework-based system of saying 'no' also helps communicate why you're saying 'no' authentically.

Saying 'no' is the biggest superpower you have.

SHOWING UP

The maximum resistance we feel towards doing anything comes right at the start.

The task ahead seems most daunting when we've made no progress towards it at all. This is why almost all advice on getting something done is to just get started. If you have already worn your running shoes and are out of the house, it is more likely that you will run. Instead of trying to motivate yourself to run five kilometres, just try getting yourself to put on your shoes and get out. If you can bring yourself to simply take that first step, following through becomes much easier.

If you've blocked time for your priorities on your calendar, just decide for yourself what the simple first step for each is. If we want to focus on deep work, maybe the first step is to put away our phones, close other distractions and sit at our desks. Turn these first steps into rituals that you do consistently. The more consistent your rituals, the better your mind becomes at knowing that it is time to focus.

Half the battle is showing up.

The other half is doing what you're supposed to do. We know that we procrastinate because of our inability to cope with our negative emotions around a task. But most people would rather admit to being busy than to being afraid. We often try to minimize the guilt of procrastination by being busy doing something else instead.

The second most important habit for successful time blocking is to treat blocked time as non-negotiable. Once we've scheduled a block for work or for a hobby, we only have two choices—use it or lose it. That is, either you spend time doing what you scheduled, or you don't do anything at all. No other projects, no reading news, no checking emails, no browsing social media or anything else if it is not on the schedule. Prolific author Neil Gaiman describes how this rule works for him.

'I think it's really just a solid rule for writers. You don't have to write. You have permission to not write, but you don't have permission to do anything else. What I love about that is I'm giving myself permission to write or not write, but writing is actually more interesting than doing nothing after a while. You sit there and you've been staring out the window now for five minutes, and it kind of loses its charm. You're going, "Well, actually, let's all write something."'

No matter how good our system of managing our to-dos and appointments, there will be days when we don't feel like starting. Like Muhammed Ali, the record-breaking boxer, once said, 'Everyone has a plan till they get punched in the face.' Our plans are often upset by our own emotions, energy levels, the weather, events around us, and many other reasons. It is on those days that we need to remember just two simple rules for keeping our promises with our past selves.

No matter what, show up.

You have permission to do nothing, but you do not have permission to do anything else.

IT IS NOT A SYSTEM IF IT ISN'T SELF-CORRECTING

Our system so far is to budget our time to reflect our priorities, say no to unimportant things, and put what's important on the calendar. These are tools to anchor where you should be spending your time. But even when we know exactly what to do, we can still feel resistance or lose focus. How we actually spend our time every day will vary from the plan.

If you can stick to the methods discussed here, you should have no trouble at all in focusing on the right things. But we know this is not how it goes. As Yogi Berra once said, 'In theory, there's no difference between theory and practice. In practice—there is.'

Self-correcting systems need a feedback loop. Our plans for where our attention should be can improve only if we know where our attention actually goes. Hence, the final piece in managing our time better is using our working memory as a daily journal. In the previous chapter, we describe Bitfulness Meditation as a journaling exercise that helps us become self-aware. We can use this exercise throughout the day to become more aware of where our time really is going.

Open up your working memory page for today and start writing about what you were just working on. Mark the time, and write a few lines about what you've done, and what you were thinking you'll do next. Don't try to be too rigid about the format, and just write down whatever is on your mind. You will be revisiting these notes later. For example,

10.00 a.m. Just finished writing an article on the N-DEAR ecosystem. It is still not finished, but I have an outline in place and the introduction is done. Will share with Shankar for feedback.

Writing down what you were just working on and how to wrap it up allows you to close the 'open loop' in your head. Every time you finish one thing or are about to start another, take a moment to make an entry in your working memory page on today's date.

10.05 a.m. I'm now starting preparation for next week's board meeting. I will first read the reports that were sent and note my comments.

Sometimes your attention will want to wander in the middle of a task. Instead of acting on your urge for distraction, get it out of your head and into your journal. By writing down your thoughts, you slow down enough to be able to not react to your instincts and choose carefully.

> *10.14 a.m. What happened to the report that was supposed to be launched last week? Must follow up with Kamya. #call #followup*

If you get distracted anyway, make it a point to spend a minute in your journal to reorient yourself before starting.

> *10.43 a.m. Was looking up that tweet by Ganesh for the article. Ended up spending 20 mins on twitter. I am now going to rewrite the first three paragraphs based on the information I just found.*

Maintaining a work journal is very useful in being able to recover from distractions. You can see your own train of thoughts and what you were up to right before you got distracted. Usually writing just a few lines allows you to remember where you were mentally and regain context that much faster.

Using your working memory as a daily journal reduces the penalties of switching contexts often. The 'system' only works if it self-corrects and adapts to your needs. Else, it is not a system, it is just a guess.

YOUR GPS, NOT YOUR BOSS

Remember, the purpose of writing down the trivial details of what you're doing day to day is not to create a record; it is to think.

The real advantage of the habit is that you start paying attention to how you actually spend your time. You become much more self-aware about how you lose time and how to recover when you do. You may realize that whenever you get a WhatsApp notification, you tend to abandon work to first reply. You may realize that you are scheduling too little (or too much) time for something important. You may be trying to do too many (or too few) things.

Instead of overthinking in the abstract, with a feedback system we can focus on more actionable details. 'Am I spending too little time with family? Am I failing at work–life balance?' to 'Did I block time for family this week? Did I show up for it?' You can take concrete steps to fix the problem by reassessing your priorities, adjusting your time budget and blocking more time for what you need to do.

Many people find it strange to put 'Dinner with spouse' or 'Change the sheets' on the calendar. They instead limit their calendar use to synchronize meetings with colleagues for work only. For some other people, the idea of planning itself is aversive. They believe they will become too restricted if so much of their day is planned and quartered. They think they are better suited to 'go with the flow'.

Your calendar isn't your boss, it is your life's GPS.

On any given day, as you navigate the distracting, noisy internet, these systems—your time budget, your schedule and your daily journal—tell you where you are in terms of progress towards your most important goals. You can still make changes every day and adapt your calendars to your mood and situation that day.

What is important is that having these systems allow you to tell if you're keeping the promises you made to yourself over the long run. In an office, your employer would hold you accountable to your responsibilities. If you shirk them, you might be reprimanded, lose pay or even your job. We don't face any such immediate consequences for the promises we make to ourselves. However, we pay for the promises we miss in terms of lost potential.

What we described in this and the previous chapter are thinking tools. They help you think clearly and help think about the things that matter. And you don't just think at work. The reasons we put meetings with others on our calendars are the same reasons we should do it for our own selves or with our loved ones. It shows us our commitments in one place so that we can make better decisions with our time. It helps us to prepare and show up for important events on schedule. It tells our loved ones we respect their time. If you feel embarrassed, you don't have to share the invite with them, but it is still useful to have it on your own calendar.

Having a system is even more critical for those who tend to go with the flow. If we make a habit of quickly capturing all tasks and appointments as they occur, this system doesn't require much upkeep. If we are in a habit of capturing everything, we can start relying on our digital systems entirely. It is a wonderful, calming feeling to know that we don't have to think about what to do next. It frees us up to go with the flow of our thoughts, without worrying about whether we're missing, forgetting or falling behind on something. It lets us be truly present in the moment.

Another common mistake is that we tend to design personal productivity systems for an ambitious version of ourselves to do the maximum number of things. We design the system for someone who always shows up, does every task in exactly the time available, takes copious notes and files everything systematically.

Instead, to have maximum peace of mind, design your personal productivity systems for your laziest self, the one who forgets to add tags, who writes 'send email' as a to-do but doesn't specify what email or to whom, and the one who will take notes but will forget where they took them. You will have more success when future-you does not expect past-you to be extremely diligent. If your system works even on days you don't feel like working much, you've made the best system.

It is very easy to start over-engineering these systems such that they become a form of distraction themselves. On the internet, this tendency even has a name—'productivity porn'. You should iterate, experiment and personalize till you find something that matches your personal workflow. Do remember that designing the perfect system is meaningless, because our lives are too dynamic and constantly evolving for there to be one perfect, static system.

Success comes from the compounding effect of consistent habits. Instead of maximizing 'productivity' or number of to-dos completed in a day, maximize the number of promises met by your future self. Building a consistent habit of reflection by using your extended mind as a mirror allows you to think clearly about your long-term goals. Most importantly, it helps you make the time to achieve them.

7

A POVERTY OF ATTENTION

ENVIRONMENTS AND BOUNDARIES

In 2004, researchers Eric Johnson and Daniel Goldstein asked an intriguing question, 'Do defaults change lives?'

Johnson and Goldstein were studying organ donation rates across Europe. They were investigating why some countries had a perpetually high rate of donations every year, whereas some had a perpetually low rate. This was very perplexing because organ donation rates in Sweden and Denmark, which were similar to each other geographically, demographically and culturally, stood at 85.9 per cent vs 4.25 per cent, respectively. The researchers ruled out all potential causes for the difference in rates, until only one remained.

Out of the eleven countries shown on this graph, all of those with high donation rates had one simple design decision. They had made organ donation the default and asked people to send a form to opt out. The countries with low organ donation rates asked people to opt in for it. Asking people to send in a form was friction enough to stop people from donating. Just making a simple change to the process could change donation rates. Or as Johnson and Goldstein put it, changing the default can save lives.

The lesson here is generalizable to more than just policy design. The design of how a choice is presented affects the choice itself. The consequences of the design are simple to understand when there is a form asking you to opt in or opt out. We make many more complex choices every day based on the information presented by our environment. If we are not mindful of our environment's influence, we might be making the wrong decisions.

THE FRICTION OF FILLING A FORM CAN COST LIVES

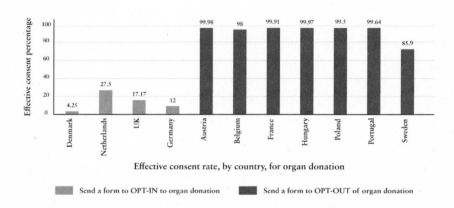

Effective consent rate, by country, for organ donation

■ Send a form to OPT-IN to organ donation   ■ Send a form to OPT-OUT of organ donation

In the purely analogue environment of the past, there was friction that would enforce some boundaries between different parts of life. Before smartphones, one was much less likely to get caught up reading a magazine article at their desk instead of working. To do that, one would have to intentionally bring a magazine to work or go out and find one. These tasks impose a significant cognitive effort and deliberate break from routine. We are likely to have paused and realized that we could read that article later. With smartphones, your friend may forward you a link to an article, and you end up reading it before you even realize you're doing it.

We can change a lot about our digital behaviour by simply changing our information environment. The information environment means the entire ecosystem of devices, apps and data that make up our extended mind. From which device we use and where we use them, to the apps on them, can be selected and configured deliberately to assist us in focusing on our goal and steering us away from distractions.

You can try this yourself if you're not convinced. Most of us carry our phones with us wherever we go, even when we're merely moving from one room in our house to another. A straightforward way to keep your phone use to the minimum when at home is to simply leave it plugged in, away from your desk, in an area where there are no chairs, beds or other seating around. If we're not comfortable while on our phones, our feet will eventually remind us to look up and go do something else.

The curse of technology available anytime, anywhere, is that we end up using it all the time, everywhere. Digital technologies that vie for our attention depend on our laziness. While they give us plenty of choices to turn distracting features off, or log out entirely, they put in a lot of friction to those choices. For example, one needs to go through a multi-step process to deactivate one's Facebook account, including providing a reason why one is shutting down. But, simply logging in reactivates the account. They choose the defaults, so the defaults are, unsurprisingly, configured to get more of our time and attention.

Every time we drop in on our screens, we end up in front of an information environment, and its design is going to affect us whether we like it or not. By default, these environments make it easy to get distracted. We need to design our environment for maximizing flow and minimizing friction.

We believe that with mindful use of technology, we can make laziness our advantage instead of our weakness. Instead of trying to fight the tendency to be lazy, we align our objectives with it. We can design an environment such that focusing on the thing we want to do is the lazy option, and slacking off is the difficult one. We can learn how to not swim upstream by splitting our personalities.

SPLIT ACCOUNTS, NOT DEVICES

There's very little that our phones, tablets and laptops can't do. We confuse that possibility for necessity.

Our devices are usually configured to have all the apps we could ever need in every context. By default, our social media is the same number of clicks away as our email on our phone, and both are available to us all the time. If we were to configure our technology mindfully, is this how it would look?

The lack of friction between these very different contexts means that at every moment, the only thing stopping us from getting distracted is our own willpower. It would be akin to trying to stay on a diet with a pocketful of our favourite candy.

As we learnt earlier, humans perform optimally when they are single-tasking with full engagement on a challenging problem. This state is also known as flow. Multitasking or switching contexts often carries a heavy cognitive penalty and breaks flow. Keeping our attention on a single task is hard if our environment is always presenting us with incoming, novel information.

One way around this problem would be to have different devices for different contexts. You could dedicate your laptop to doing work only and your smartphone to personal browsing. Or you could buy additional devices. However, buying additional devices soon becomes unwieldy, not to mention expensive. Until brain implants become a reality, we will still need to access the digital world through a physical device. For convenience, you want fewer devices to manage and charge, not more. This bottleneck is one that you can use to your advantage.

Nandan already divides his devices the way he wants to divide his time. He only does work on his PC. When he's on the computer, he's working. He checks his email for a long stretch twice a day, first thing in the morning and last thing at night. He batches emails that he has to send so as to not get lost in his inbox often. He consumes a curated selection of eight news subscriptions every day on his iPad and, occasionally, Twitter. When he wants to relax, he uses the same iPad for Netflix, Amazon Prime Video, and Disney+ Hotstar. His phone is for him to make calls and send texts. His phone is always on silent since this allows him to think. He has no email on his phone and no other apps that bombard him with information. The only game he plays is FreeCell (badly).

Admittedly, having multiple devices and the discipline to follow through on separating them is a tough ask. It may work for you, as it does for Nandan. Instead of having multiple devices, we can also have the same device configured for different modes by managing our identities. As users, we don't pay particular attention to how we manage our identities. We tend to use the defaults suggested by our technology. We think in terms of usernames, passwords, accounts and profiles, but managing our identity can be much richer than that. Designed well, managing our identity can be extremely effective at helping us stay in control of our attention and manage our privacy.

On most laptops and smartphones, one can set up multiple user accounts. Each account created acts as a completely new and independent virtual space. This simple trick lets us effectively have many virtual devices, even when the physical device remains the same.

With multiple virtual devices, we can configure each identity thoughtfully for a purpose. We can give each account a 'personality'. For example, if you are a writer, other than your usual account, you could have an account on your computer which has no other apps except the word processor you use. To do anything else, you'd first have to log out and then log in to another account.

Instead of exerting our willpower every single moment, we can invest time once in designing these accounts purposefully. On a daily basis, we simply need to choose which 'personality' we need to be in now. If we've configured these different contexts well, the opportunities for getting distracted reduce significantly.

Splitting your personality is essentially a pre-commitment strategy. These are also known as 'Ulysses pacts' because of the use of this concept in Homer's poem Odyssey. The hero Ulysses is sailing his way back home, but he must pass the Sirens. The Sirens were infamous for singing an irresistible song that led men to their deaths in the treacherous sea. Ulysses plugged the ears of his crew with wax. He instructed them to tie him to the mast and to stay the course no matter what he says in the future. Ulysses knew that his present self before being enthralled by the Sirens was a better decision-maker than his future self. He set up his environment accordingly.

In the digital world, you can lock yourself out of your social media accounts by logging out. Or simply give your phone to a loved one and ask them not to give it back to you till you finish some important task. Some pre-commitment strategies themselves are either high friction or not rigid enough to be useful. Splitting your personality lets you implement pre-commitments in a flexible manner.

People are often hesitant about pre-commitment strategies. They look at these pacts as inflexible, rigid constraints that limit freedom. A mindset shift is required to appreciate their power. These rigid boundaries do not keep us locked inside or restrict our freedom. Instead, these boundaries are meant to keep the constant din and noise outside so that we can be free to really focus.

Writers have often complained of procrastination. It might console you to know that even the best, most celebrated authors suffer the same problems as you do. The problem predates modern technology. Victor Hugo, the famous French novelist and poet, had signed a contract in 1829 to write a book he had titled *The Hunchback of Notre Dame*. Hugo spent the next twelve months entertaining guests, taking up side projects, and generally doing things other than writing the book that would eventually make him famous.

In September 1830, his publisher got furious with him and gave him an incredibly challenging six-month deadline to submit the novel by February of 1831. Hugo knew he was prone to being social, and this was his biggest temptation. He then made a Ulysses pact. He packed all his clothes and gave them to his attendant to keep away from his chambers. But for a shawl, Hugo was completely naked. Thus, with no option to go out or receive guests, Hugo worked on his novel non-stop.

He finished the 1,87,000-word novel two weeks early.

CHOOSING HOW TO SPLIT

How should we design our personalities?

For a lot of people, the primary objective is to get back some work–life balance. We're often Facebooking at work and emailing at home. You might be tempted to create two profiles for home and office. But, this distinction is not as clear-cut as it first seems. Even in the office context, activities like emails and group chats can be a source of distraction and procrastination. We end up doing 'research' for two hours, when we should've written what we knew already.

Our recommended approach is to not base these identities on any extrinsic categories like office, school, personal, etc. Instead, it is much more useful to base these identities on intrinsic motivations and the tasks we want to accomplish.

Consider two environments. The first is a library. Everyone is quiet, the room is well-lit and there's plenty of desks and chairs. The other is a party in a living room. The TV is playing a cricket match, some of your friends are talking in a group in one corner, and loud music is playing in the background. If you had to do a hard task that requires your focus, such as figuring out your personal savings plan or making an excel model for work, in which environment do you think you'd get quality work done?

Even though we understand this about physical spaces, we make no effort to extend this logic to our digital spaces. Our computers are configured to be more like the party than the library. Every distraction—group chat with friends, videos via Netflix, or memes via social media—is always just one new tab away.

As Herbert Simon said, 'a wealth of information creates a poverty of attention'. We believe that certain activities such as email, social media or just general browsing will always contain extraneous or novel information. Our brains are wired to shift attention to these. Hence, these apps are inherently more prone to derailing our focus.

Instead of categories like personal or work, we recommend splitting identity based on the quality and type of attention you need for the task. Since attention is inversely proportional to the information in your environment, you can design these 'personalities' to regulate how much information you receive.

Specifically, every time we turn on any of our devices, we think there are three modes of attention that we should decide between. These three modes are

1. Create
2. Curate
3. Communicate

The Create mode is one where we want to bring our full and deep attention to the task at hand. We want no distractions in this mode.

We want to be Ulysses tied to the mast, not changing course, no matter what the Sirens are singing. What one wants in this mode is to create—to make meaningful progress on the goals that matter.

The Curate mode is the opposite of the Create mode. Whether we're looking to get inspired, catch up on the news or simply take a break, we seek content to consume. But we often get swept up in consumption. What one wants to do is curate—to be deeply immersed in the content—while still being in control at a high level of the quality and quantity of what we consume.

The Communicate mode is our planning and management mode. Emails, instant messages, group chats and other inboxes contain a stream of information that we *must* deal with. These streams contain a mix of signal and noise. Some are urgent, some are important, many are neither. The critical task is to quickly decide how one wants to deal with this information. In the Communicate mode, we want to be able to parse a large amount of information, but not get too caught up in any one thing. Instead, we want to strategize and communicate. We want to be able to respond to incoming requests from others with clear responses. We also want to communicate to our future selves the shifting priorities to help us rethink what we should do next.

The next three chapters are deep dives into how we can set up these three modes. We also go over strategies on how to split your time between them. But first, we want to dive deeper into why we believe you should be splitting your personality by mode of attention.

WHY SPLIT BY MODE OF ATTENTION

To appreciate the difference between these modes, think about the 'flow' of information in each of these environments. We are in a state of flow when the kind of information environment we are in is complementary to the mode of attention we want to inhabit.

In Create mode, there is no incoming 'flow' of information. Instead, there is a still reservoir of knowledge—notes and documents from your working memory and long-term storage. From that, only draw what you need for the task at hand. You can choose to work on that important presentation for the office or on writing a thoughtful letter to a friend. What's important is that there is nothing to pull you away. This helps you create without getting distracted.

In the Curate mode, one deals with the rapids—information streams that are too voluminous and forceful to be tamed, such as social media or newsletters. Just like white-water rapids, these streams are often shallow and fast-moving. Getting on them can be a thrill, but keep going long enough and you will get wet, fall over or capsize, no matter what your level of experience and expertise. You want to be able to curate the best and consume with intent, instead of consuming mindlessly.

In Communicate mode, we deal with dams. There is an incoming flow that we cannot ignore, but at the same time, we cannot be driven by its rhythms. We let it collect in our inboxes and deal with that information on our own time and on our own terms. We want to be able to segregate the urgent and the important from the noise.

There is no hierarchy between the three modes. The deliberate boundaries between these modes help us create thoughtful information environments that support us in what we're trying to do. For a balanced life, you will probably be spending time in each mode.

Splitting personalities reduces the amount of cognitive overhead required to focus on the present. It brings a sense of calmness while immersed in any given task. This is as true of curation as it is for creation. We find that we tend to enjoy our time engaging with curated content when it is done deliberately at a time of our choosing.

Most importantly, attaching each mode to a different identity creates a valuable moment of pause. Before we begin doing anything, we need to login to our computers or our phones. We now start this process with a conscious decision. Given our energy levels and the time we have and the list of things we need to do, what is it that we feel like doing right now? Are we going to Create, Curate or Communicate?

In the next three chapters, we go over how to set up and use each one of these personalities in detail.

8

CREATE MODE

PRINCIPLES OF CREATE MODE

The Create mode is where your deep work happens.

You want this to be an environment where you can easily get into flow. Hence, this is where you go when you want to work on any project that demands quality, focused attention. Whether you need to do accounts for work or write a poem for pleasure, to be in flow, you need to be deeply engrossed. Remember, the conditions to enable the flow state are a clear goal, immediate feedback and a balance of skill and challenge. As long as we're able to focus on our most important goal and have a clear objective for our time, we have everything we need to trigger the flow state.

The real challenge is friction. Both external and internal triggers could derail us from our state of relaxed concentration. In Create mode, we want to block the internet by default. We want to allow our future self only very specific tunnels to those sites and apps that are absolutely critical to focused work. Nothing else is allowed by default.

Some of you may have cringed as you read that. Just the thought of not having the internet for even a few minutes is worrying for some people. The Create mode is just one of the modes on our computers. Getting out of that mode and on to the internet will always be possible. We're just trying to make it harder, so that we do it less often when trying to focus.

Now that we know what we're trying to achieve, let's set up our Create personality accordingly.

SETTING UP CREATE MODE

The first step is to choose the primary device for Create mode.

For many of us, our primary device for doing deep work would be our laptops. Some of us can do all our work entirely from a smartphone. The strategies that follow can be applied to either. However, choose your primary device carefully to make Creating easier.

If you can work from either a laptop or a smartphone, it might be worth considering moving to a laptop simply for ergonomic reasons. Most android phones can support multiple accounts, but iPhones do not. If you can only work from your iPhone, consider purchasing an additional device to separate your deep work from the rest of your day.

On the device that you have chosen to be your primary device, create a new user account. The process to do this varies depending on your operating system. The Appendix explains how you can do this on the most popular ones. Once activated, you will notice that this account is as good as a new computer or phone. From this point on, you need to be extremely careful about what you install in this account. Do install the basics such as the calendar app and the app you use as your working memory. If you use cloud storage for your long-term memory, make sure you have access to that too.

Before you add anything else to this account, it might be worth writing down in your working memory what you plan on doing in the Create mode. This will help you be more thoughtful about the apps to install. You must show ruthlessness in saying no to all possible sources of distraction or any app that constantly has novel information. Even the ones that may look like work at first. This especially includes your email, instant messaging apps and group chat apps. Your default should be to not install any new tool or app in this account, unless it explicitly helps you considerably in doing deep work.

The Create mode is a virtual environment, but creating is a physical activity. We want to help our body and mind align with our extended mind by changing our physical environment too.

If you work consistently from an office or from home, try to sit in the same place on the same desk every day. If possible, at the same time too. These clues help your brain understand that it is time to focus. Do make sure that this space is set up to be both comfortable and ergonomic. Bad ergonomics can cause repetitive strain injuries that can affect parts of our fingers, wrists and elbows, which can cause further complications in our necks and backs.

Once you have the basics set up, it is time to start blocking out distractions.

DEALING WITH EXTERNAL DISTRACTIONS

No matter what your profession, at some point, you probably need a web browser for your work. Web browsers are a terrible sink of your attention since you have literally all the world's information at your fingertips. The simple way out is to make a Ulysses pact using a website blocker.

Website blockers are apps that prevent us from accessing distracting websites. Most have a pre-populated list of common distracting websites like social media, news sites, gaming sites, etc. We can add the ones that are our personal sinkholes of time.

Most of these blockers allow us to work in sessions, blocking these websites for certain times of the day. We recommend that for the Create profile, you block these distracting websites permanently. You will need to leave a short 'maintenance window' when the blocker isn't running so that you can change the settings as needed. Also, lock the settings that allow you to quit the session in the middle. Tie yourself to the mast.

Your particular profession may require you to look up things online often. Lawyers need to find judgments and programmers need to look up documentation. As far as possible, use tools that download these datasets offline. Where this isn't possible, you can also whitelist websites. That is, the blocker will block everything except these specific reference sites. Try to use this option sparingly.

As far as possible, completely block social media and other distracting apps that are fuelled by attention. For a few professions, however, social media is needed for work. HR professionals may need to access LinkedIn. Journalists may need to look up specific tweets on

Twitter. If you block social media aggressively even though your job requires it, pretty soon you will abandon the system of split personalities.

Instead, make a distinction between personal social media and that which you need to look up for work. Whitelist only the ones you need for work. You can also use specific tools such as the browser extension 'News Feed Eradicator', which blocks out the news feed section of most social media. It removes your feed and replaces it with a quote reminding you that you do not want to get lost.

Further, use your identity on social media to your advantage. Stay logged out of the social network where it is possible to view the content anonymously, for example, Twitter or Reddit. You will still be able to access the content you need, but staying logged out prevents the platforms from tracking and knowing your identity. Without knowing your identity, they can't show you personalized content from friends, family or topics of interest that can take you down rabbit holes.

DEALING WITH INTERNAL DISTRACTIONS

Many people have an aversion to software that permanently blocks their access to the internet. Some have used it and eventually abandoned it because they were too ambitious in their blocking. In our system, the blocking applies locally to the Create personality. If you really need access to a specific website urgently, you can log out from that personality and log in to something else.

However, nine times out of ten, it might be a better idea to delay gratification and not actually switch modes. Our internet-connected devices make it extremely low-friction to simply switch contexts and tasks to follow our every whim instantly. You want to put some time and distance between when you have a desire and when you act on it.

Most times, this pause will help you realize that what you wanted to look up was simply another way of getting distracted. But your brain won't let you pause unless you get the 'open loop' out of your head and into a system.

This is when you should use your working memory to make a note of whatever was distracting you. If you're already using your working memory as a journal, you will have a series of entries.

You can simply write down whatever is bothering you in your journal in your working memory. When writing into the working memory, don't worry too much about organizing or even about writing clearly. Simply write till the distracting thought is out of your head so that you can go back to creating.

Remember, like Ulysses, when you entered the Create mode, you had a plan to focus on what's truly important. Instead of using willpower, the idea is to simply let your environment prevent you from making a costly error.

We will learn how to process these distracting thoughts you just wrote down in the Communicate Mode.

USE NOTIFICATIONS MINDFULLY

The cocktail party effect states that our subconscious is constantly filtering what we hear and deciding what we pay attention to. Even when we are in a crowded party, with many overlapping conversations and sounds, if someone says our name, we stop mid-sentence to look over. A loud explosion, or the sound of our own name, causes our attention to switch rapidly to the source.

Many scientists who study the link between attention and smartphones now concur that smartphones have come to occupy a 'privileged attentional space'. They are as powerful a signal to our brain as someone calling out our name at a party. We respond to it immediately, dropping whatever it is we're doing, like we would to a tap on the shoulder. This is quite a lot of power for any device to have over us.

By default, our smartphones and computers exploit this 'privileged attentional space' via notifications.

Turning off all non-essential notifications is the simplest but most effective intervention you can make to reduce the overwhelm in your life. You can turn them off completely for Create mode, but some of these strategies may be useful more generally. Turning off notifications from non-essential apps stops you from losing attention to apps, such as games or e-commerce, which you want to use only when you intend.

Switching off notifications can also backfire. If we are anxious about missing messages from colleagues or family, we may end up unlocking our phone more to check if we've received a text when notifications are off. Hence, we believe that you need to mindfully architect your notifications to suit your context.

1. TURN OFF ALL TIME-INSENSITIVE NOTIFICATIONS

The first thing to do is to turn off all notifications that don't really require our immediate attention. Most people who have done this report feeling less stressed and having a better sense of control over their time. This is an action that won't take two minutes to set up but the pay-offs are tremendous. The hard part of this exercise consists in deciding which notifications are truly urgent, and should be kept on.

We suggest starting by turning everything off. Let your calendar and phone notifications pass through as these require your immediate attention. As you experiment with this for a few days, you'll realize which other notifications need your urgent attention.

If you haven't already turned off all notifications on your phone, do it now. From today onwards, every time a new notification appears on your screen, and it appears useless, don't just dismiss it. Take an extra second to block all future notifications of that type from that app by long-pressing the notification.

2. BATCH THE TIME-SENSITIVE
NOTIFICATIONS YOU CAN'T TURN OFF

Notifications can be useful in one very narrow way. A lot of us are in the habit of checking text messages. With all notifications blocked, we do not know if there are new messages without opening the app. We might just tend to go overboard in picking up our phones and checking the instant messaging apps every few minutes, even when no new messages have arrived.

On the other hand, if we do turn on notifications, when new messages do arrive, they will keep bothering us at times we're trying to focus. One way to deal with this problem is to get an app to batch the notifications. All the notifications will be sent at fixed periodic intervals of our choice. For example, you could choose to get all your email notifications at 11 a.m. and then only again at 4 p.m. Or you could get all your text notifications five minutes past every hour. This way, instead of constantly checking in, you can quickly glance at your phone to see if it requires your attention.

If you do batch notifications, remember it is still critical to block the useless ones. You can block notifications entirely from useless apps, but at times, you can also block specific notifications from within an app. In WhatsApp, muting a group or a sender prevents notifications from them while still allowing notifications from others to be batched. See the Appendix for a list of such apps under the heading 'Batch your Notifications'.

3. USE DO-NOT-DISTURB MODE TO SCREEN NOTIFICATIONS.

Due to the nature of their work, some people may simply be unable to avoid turning notifications off completely. If you're a doctor, then maybe calls from your office are critical for you to attend. Almost all phones come with a 'focus mode' or 'do not disturb mode' where your notifications do not ring and only specific callers or messages are screened through. Learn where this option is on your phone, and make a shortcut to it. Use it often!

MAKE YOUR PHONE FOCUSED

Our problems don't end with simply managing notifications. Our smartphones have slowly turned into everything-devices and it is very easy to lose context.

The University of Texas study from Chapter 4 told us that people lost cognitive capacity to their phones, even when it was *switched off but in front of them*. If you can create on your laptop only, consider simply putting away your phone, out of sight while you're creating. You won't be spending all your time in this mode, so you can afford to stay away from your phone. But if you need to have your phone on you, you can still choose to make it a more focused device.

1. SPLIT IDENTITY ON YOUR PHONE TOO

Most Android phones also allow us to create new user accounts on our phones. Just like we did with our laptops, it is a great idea to create a second account on our smartphones for focused work only. For most phones, this is done in the phone's settings, under an option called 'Users and Accounts'.

It is as good as getting a second phone, with a fresh install. When creating this account, you will be asked to login to a Google account. Make sure the email you use to login is *not* your primary email account. Using your primary account means you'll be able to check your email from this identity as well, which we want to avoid. Get a fresh email so that this second identity is completely air-gapped from your primary identity. You should now be very intentional about which apps you add to this account.

Ideally, this profile should only be able to make calls, check your calendar and take notes. Any utilities that do not have an infinite feed of new information are okay to keep. This could mean maps, taxi apps, listening to music, etc., are ok. But email, instant messages and others are not. Do not install any games or other possible distractions on this second account. Just like you did on your laptop, make sure this identity has no extraneous apps that become time-sucks.

You can also set everything from ringtone to do-not-disturb settings differently, without affecting your main account. Try to stay in this account whenever you're in Create mode. If you notice yourself on some apps that are making you lose time, delete them from this identity and reinstall them in your primary account if needed.

Switching between identities is easy, but not smooth. This friction is intentional and will help you stay in the right mode.

2. DISTRACTION BLOCKING APPS

We strongly recommend getting a website blocking app that syncs with your smartphone as well. The appendix lists some of these apps that allow you to start a focus session on one or more of your devices simultaneously. When you're trying to be focused in the Create mode, the software should block distracting apps on your phone as well. This way, even if you do accidentally or out of habit try to open a distracting website on your phone, it will stop you from doing so.

If you do follow Step 1 above and create a second identity for the Create mode on your phone, we strongly recommend blocking all websites by default on this profile at all times. The advantage of creating a second identity is that most software services treat this as a completely new device. You can set blocking rules for the Create mode differently from the other user identities on your phone. If you really need access, you can switch accounts. We're trying to increase friction just enough to block the unintentional, automatic behaviours that we have learnt.

3. CHANGE YOUR HOME SCREEN

The home screen was designed to let us access all our apps quickly. At least for the Create mode, this is the wrong principle. We want to be able to only access the apps that let us create easily and increase friction for those that don't.

On Android phones, you can change your home screen to be significantly less distracting by changing the default home screen to a minimalistic launcher. See the Appendix for some suggestions. Even if you don't change the launcher itself, do remove all shortcuts to distracting apps from your home screen.

MAKE IT PERSONAL

Finally, make your Create mode personalized to your needs.

The Create mode is your personal mute button for the internet. Don't be afraid to ruthlessly block websites, apps and other distractions that you find too tempting from this mode. Whenever things get overwhelming, you can simply log in to this account to block out the noise.

Customize the theme on this account to make sure it looks visually different from your other accounts. Change the wallpaper to something that motivates you. It could be a quote, a scene, a goal, your role model, but anything that is deeply personal to you. You could simply write in a large font what your most important goal is. This cues your brain into remembering that when you're here, you should be in a state of flow, working towards what's important to you.

Remind yourself not just of what you need to create but why you're doing it.

Standing at the base of any hill, the path ahead always seems formidable. True motivation comes from progress. While it sounds like a strict set of rules, remember that the Create mode is ultimately about making progress on your most important goals. Over time, you will actually enjoy coming back to this distraction-free space because you will get addicted to the feeling of progress you create when you aren't distracted.

The Create Mode maximizes flow, and minimizes friction. If you spend time in Create mode every day as a ritual, your brain will learn to be focused at that point every time. You will see tremendous returns on the habit. After all, in a distracted world, true focus is a superpower.

9

COMMUNICATE MODE

PRINCIPLES OF COMMUNICATE MODE

We deliberately left out things like emails, instant messages and other such communication tools from the Create mode. Whether email, chat, group messages or even your own notes, you constantly have to deal with new information, tasks and decisions. We will refer to all of these generically as inboxes consisting of items. If we don't have a plan for dealing with this new information, it is easy to get lost in the deluge. We recommend creating a whole new personality on your devices for these 'inboxes' we call the Communicate mode.

Most inboxes are designed to simply collect all items that come their way and order them by recency. This may not reflect your priorities or the urgency of the tasks. A bill that is due in twenty days is displayed equally prominently as an urgent work thread that needs your input by tomorrow. Given a menu of items to choose from, our mind will wander to the easier ones that do not require us to exert cognitive effort. We start reading newsletters during work because they are in our email inbox. We push tasks that raise unpleasant emotional responses onto our future selves. Unresolved items don't just stay in our inbox, they also remain an 'open loop' in our minds, becoming a source of latent stress.

The meta-task of dealing with an inbox is different from the task of dealing with any particular item in that inbox. Instead of trying to switch between the contexts of dealing with our inboxes and dealing with the items in our inboxes, when in the Communicate mode, we should be focused on one thing only.

Getting to Inbox Zero.

INTRODUCING INBOX ZERO

Inbox Zero is a very popular strategy to deal with emails that many on the internet abide by. It is inspired by the extremely popular 4D Time Management method prescribed by David Allan, author of the massive bestseller *Getting Things Done*. The basic tenets can be extended to any sort of inbox—whether instant messages, group chats or any other.

In a nutshell, the Inbox Zero strategy requires one to be disciplined about going through inboxes regularly, and each time, getting to zero items pending. This is achieved by processing items in the inbox, one by one, without skipping, till one gets to zero items pending.

'Processing' here means following a simple pre-defined algorithm. Each item must either be Delegated, Done, Deferred, Documented or Deleted. Based on the urgency of the item and the effort required to deal with it, choose from one of the following options:

- **Delegate** to someone else if the task is more relevant to them.
- **Do** the item immediately, ONLY if it can be done in under two minutes.
- **Defer** doing it to a specific time by putting it on your calendar.
- **Document** it in your working memory if it contains information that might be useful later.
- **Delete** (or Archive, if you want to retain a copy) the item from your inbox if it doesn't require any action or is no longer relevant.

The central idea always is to have a well-defined, limited set of choices for how to process each item in your inbox. Each choice should not take too long to execute. Do NOT leave items pending in the inbox. Also, one feels a clear sense of completion and achievement when one gets to zero.

The specific algorithm for your own inbox can be modified as per need and type of inbox. Inbox Zero applies to all categories of inboxes, even if the apps don't call them that. For example, Tanuj religiously archives his conversations on WhatsApp. WhatsApp and other direct messaging tools can be overwhelming because conversations online don't really seem to end. Every new reply feels like it requires a reply too. A conversation then slowly degrades into single emojis or generic *lol*s. Instead, use the archive button to take it out of your inbox, and tell yourself that the conversation has ended. Having a visual representation of no open threads is helpful to bring calm to our minds.

Some user-hostile platforms have actually not enabled or removed the ability to archive. One can still use the delete chat option. A lot of people are uncomfortable with deleting chats. In which case, ask your friends to move the conversation over to other channels that you do prefer. Having fewer active chats or threads ensures we don't get lost in a rabbit hole or stretch a conversation.

When cleaning our inboxes, we want to stay focused on the act of triaging rather than getting deep and solving any particular item. You want to have your attention focused on high-level executive decisions around processing.

The Inbox Zero strategy is very aligned to the pre-conditions of flow we discussed in Chapter 4. It has a clear goal—getting to zero. The set of choices or rules to attain these goals are well-defined. The feedback is immediate—one can see the unprocessed/unread count dropping towards zero in real-time. Inbox Zero turns processing emails or tasks from an amorphous chore into a more well-defined, almost-fun activity.

Inbox Zero is easy to maintain if you do it consistently. However, it is hard if you don't do it already or only do it sporadically. If you can't naturally get to zero, feel free to declare bankruptcy.

DECLARE BANKRUPTCY

For many people, getting to Inbox Zero can be daunting because of the number of items that you already have pending in your inbox. Most often, people tend to have unread emails from weeks ago. Those who have to-do lists also tend to have a lot of residual tasks from long ago. For all of these, feel free to declare bankruptcy.

Declaring bankruptcy is the act of allowing yourself to fall short on your inbox obligations. Bankruptcy is accepting that it is time to let go of the 12,478 unread emails that, to be honest, you were never going to get to anyway. Specifically, this is how you go about declaring inbox bankruptcy.

1. Ensure your inbox is sorted by recency.
2. Start by completely archiving items more than a month old. There is nothing special about one month. You can choose two months or just seven days, depending on the state of your inbox and how relevant the items are to you.
3. Next, scan the remaining items, and star only the ones that seem worthy of retaining.
4. Archive the remaining non-starred items.
5. Now process through the starred items using the Inbox Zero Algorithm and get to zero.

Newsletters are one common reason why email inboxes get overwhelmed. Newsletters are more suited for 'feeds' such as social media, rather than 'inboxes' such as your email. If you do subscribe to more than a couple of newsletters, consider creating a completely new email account for them. Whenever you're subscribing to a newsletter, use this new newsletter-only email ID rather than your personal or work email ID. This way you can deal with those feeds in the Curate mode, rather than in the Communicate mode.

Declaring bankruptcy is almost always less drastic than we believe. Do not be afraid to use this as often as you need. If you're thinking about bankruptcy, you probably need to do it. But do try to use this moment to reflect on what you need to do to prevent this next time? Do you not check email regularly? Should you be unsubscribing to some emails or groups? Should your work team move some discussions away from group chats to email or vice versa?

So declare bankruptcy if you need to, and then, let's set up the Communicate mode on our devices based on the ideas of Inbox Zero.

SETTING UP THE COMMUNICATE MODE

The first thing you want to do is to create another identity on your devices for the Communicate mode. Make sure that you have the basic apps installed first. As a reminder, this includes:

- Your notes app for your working memory.
- Your calendar app for your time blocks and tasks.
- Website blockers to prevent distractions.

Install all the apps you need to manage your inboxes. This includes, but is not restricted to:

- Email
- Instant messaging
- Direct messages from social media
- Group chats
- Tasks
- Any other app that functions as an inbox you care about

Where possible, try to use a single app to manage all your different services rather than using a browser. For example, most modern email applications let us manage multiple email ids. This way we get a unified inbox across all our email inboxes. Similarly, software such as Rambox lets us see a unified inbox across all our messaging apps. See Appendix for a list of such apps.

You also want to make sure that you do NOT install any apps that may distract you. Do set up the website blockers to block your personal time-sinks. If you need access to social media, try to make sure you have blocked the newsfeed at least. Try not to login to social media from this personality at all.

Unlike in the Create mode, your smartphones are actually well-suited for the Communicate mode. The mobile user interface makes implementing Inbox Zero on smartphones easy. Most inbox apps allow us to use swipe gestures to archive, delete, etc. We can make them a part of our Inbox Zero routine. We can even choose to respond to emails or messages only from our phones, forcing ourselves to be quick about it.

YOUR WORKING MEMORY IS AN INBOX TOO

We recommended creating a working memory where every thought would land up before you process it. We also recommended that when you're trying to focus on any one task, write down any unrelated distracting thoughts that occur in your working memory.

Your working memory is an inbox too. But it starts looking like a hodgepodge of ideas, thoughts, to-dos, links to content and other such items. What does Inbox Zero on your working memory look like?

The specific algorithm for processing items in your working memory is not very different from regular Inbox Zero. You go through your working memory line by line, and process each thought. If the thought requires action, you can add the task to your calendar, on a corresponding time block.

But often the action you take to process an item in your working memory will be to clarify and 'describe' the thought better. As you go through each item, ask if this thought is written clearly enough for your future self to understand. If you come back to this thought two months later, will it still make sense to you? Does it have all the relevant tags you need so that you are able to find it in the future?

For example, you may have written down 'Interesting mail and article from Sanjay re: startup. Should read about health AI, known founder. Are there more?'

You can then translate this into 'Sanjay Jain sent an interesting article (https://..) about a #healthcare #startup called detect.ai. They are working on an automated #cancer detecting #AI starting with early detection of breast cancer. The founder is Deepak Singh, who has worked previously in Manipal Hospital.'

You may even want to add a task on your calendar to research more such start-ups. As you can see, it is much more likely that the second message will show up in one of your searches. It will also be saved in your daily page in your working memory, grouped by context.

Treating our working memory as an inbox allows us to take two chances at storing our thoughts. This gives us some leeway during the initial capture. We don't have to get every little tag and detail correctly in the first go. Our focus should be on getting the thought out of our heads, so that we can free up our minds for whatever we're doing now.

The second pass helps better crystallize our thoughts for future use. It shapes our working memory into a formidable store of knowledge, without having to pre-decide a rigid organizational structure. The tags you choose can help you create connections so that future retrieval is easier.

YOUR COMMUNICATION PLAN

A lot of people believe that if they are not constantly on top of their email or instant messages, they will lose out on some precious opportunity.

There are some jobs where this kind of responsiveness is probably warranted. If you are a day trader, having the right information at the right time could be the difference between losing or saving money. It is highly probable though that your job is not like a day trader's.

Checking your email once or maybe twice a day suffices for most jobs, and checking your instant messages once every couple of hours at best. What the exact frequency should be depends on your specific role and responsibilities. It is highly likely though that we're doing it more often than really required.

We tend to overlook the real costs of this habit. Imagine how much more focused time you would have if you weren't breaking the flow to check email very often. Imagine all the things you could've gotten done sooner if you weren't switching contexts between social media and work.

If you use time blocking, set up fixed times to check your inboxes. Try and only use your Communicate personality within this time block and try to get to Inbox Zero. If you finish early, you can reward yourself. Spend the rest of the time block on whatever distraction you like. Overall, whether you check your email every ten minutes or once a day, you're likely to go through the same amount of email in a day. But when you batch them and focus on Inbox Zero, you spend a lot less time on each email.

Often people can't switch off their phones, because they worry about missing critical communication from their colleagues. Even though none of us explicitly asked for it, we have inadvertently ended up creating unhealthy expectations about response times. Because we're always connected, we feel the pressure to reply. More often than not, this pressure is self-imposed.

The real problem is that we have not set expectations clearly.

Add a little note to your email signature that lays out your own personal communication preference. For example, 'I usually read emails within 3 days and respond to each item. If it's urgent, call'. You can even put a similar message on your WhatsApp or Slack status.

Like with any other problem, if you're overwhelmed by emails or texts, 80 per cent of the problem will come down to 20 per cent of the actors. Most people are respectful and will comply with your instructions on how to communicate. You only need to put in effort to set expectations with these 20 per cent bad actors.

You can prepare a saved, polite template to send to someone who texts instead of emailing or vice-versa. 'Hi, could you please make sure this is sent on my work email john@work.com and not text next time? I'm unable to keep track and this may result in something important being missed or overlooked.' You'll be surprised at how few times you actually have to do this once you start communicating clearly.

It is easier to set expectations with people messaging you one on one. The harder problem is in social settings and groups. Group culture is hard to change once it's set. If you're overwhelmed by too many group texts, find the noisiest group chats and mute or exit them. You don't need to be present in all conversations.

If you can't exit, find whoever is posting the most on them, and message them privately to request them to slow down. Alternatively, make a duplicate group with the same members that are 'Announcements Only'. Meaning, these groups must be strictly used for important announcements only, no memes, forwards or 'good morning' messages should be allowed. Remove those that don't comply.

In some workplaces, the problem is systemic. Everyone is in one large chat group, and everyone is expected to be available all the time.

People CC everyone in their email chains because they don't want to be accused of leaving someone out. Everyone's inboxes are flooded, but individual employees don't want to be the ones to call it out, because they don't want to be seen as the ones complaining.

If you feel this way about your workplace, you may want to talk to your colleagues one-on-one first to check if they feel the same way too. If others are also feeling overwhelmed by the state of affairs, then a change in how the office communicates may be required. Usually, communication culture devolves because no one attempted to design it mindfully. Like the emperor's new clothes, these broken systems chug along till someone stands up and points out the obvious. Voice your opinion along with others who feel this way, and you'll be surprised how many people agree.

No one wants to work all the time. But in today's distracting world, even leisure can't hold our undivided attention. To really switch off and play, needs a *little* bit of work. That's why you need Curate mode.

10

CURATE MODE

PRINCIPLES OF CURATE MODE

The Curate mode is better defined by what it is not. It is where we are *not* doing deep work and *not* communicating.

In an always-connected world, disconnecting needs to be a deliberate act. We need a space to simply be ourselves. This is the Curate mode.

When you know what you're really looking for, the internet can be a wonderful place. It has amazing content in any format you can ask for. Whether text, images, audio or video, content is available in many languages, and large parts of it for free. You feel the satisfaction of having learnt something that you intended to learn. Or simply be entertained.

It is important, however, that you do *not* use the Curate mode only to mindlessly consume.

If you're simply checking your feeds out of habit, without any self-awareness of why you're doing it, you're much more likely to end up zoning out. You end up feeling like you wasted time. The content you consumed was probably not low-quality; it was simply not what you *intended* to do at the time.

The internet is an infinite content-generation machine. Most of this content is delivered to you through infinite 'feeds'. Social media, news sites, public discussion forums, podcast subscriptions, video channels—all are feeds. Even newsletters are feeds, just less frequent than the others. The totality of such feeds is an endless buffet of content. There is no way in which you can consume all of it. But just because you can't consume all of it, doesn't mean your brain doesn't try. Whether a buffet of food or content, you tend to over consume when presented with that kind of variety and choice.

How does one manage this information overload to only get to the best and most relevant content?

The short answer is you can't. There is no 'best' content. There is no way in which you can ensure that your feeds only contain high-quality relevant or timely content that you will definitely enjoy. There will always be noise. Content creators are human, and their quality varies too. Our taste changes with time, so does the definition of 'relevant'.

Besides, even if you could somehow select 'best' feeds or have Artificial Intelligence select them for you, then all the content would probably be too narrowly selected from a series of topics you definitely care about. You would lose the serendipity you get from stumbling into something novel, interesting or weird that you would never have selected for yourself.

Instead of looking for ways to get only relevant content, we can ask a related, but different question.

How do we make the most out of our time when consuming content, so that we walk away feeling intellectually, emotionally or spiritually nourished?

This framing acknowledges that there is no 'best' in this infinite buffet. What we want to do is align what we are consuming to what we need in the moment. The objective isn't to manage our content or feeds, but to make mindful use of our time.

The way to do that is to set up your Curate personality and forget your passwords.

SETTING UP CURATE MODE

If you've been following the recommendations so far, you should have three identities on your device by now. You should have created two new users for the Create and Communicate modes. Your original user account can be your Curate mode. After that, you can begin by removing all the software that you do not plan on using in this mode, especially any work-related or communication apps. If you use a separate newsletter-only email ID, you may want to set that up here.

You will want to use a website blocker here too. However, instead of blocking social media, news, games and other such sites, you may want to lock yourself out from doing serious work in this account. This 'anti-block' helps build the habit of doing focused work only in the Create or Communicate mode, and not in the Curate mode.

As we mentioned before, there is no hierarchy to these modes. The reason we have an explicit Curate mode is not just so that you can't be distracted when you're working. It is also so that you don't start working when you're supposed to be relaxing. You should aggressively block out work from this personality, just as you blocked distractions from the Create mode.

The point of these personalities is to create boundaries between the different parts of your life. While we all acknowledge that the internet is distracting us from important work, we also need to acknowledge how it is distracting us from true leisure.

When you are in this account, you are here to spend time on leisure activities guilt-free. Feel free to install whatever you need. From now on, any new apps you want to try, games, or other software can be installed here.

Now that you have three modes, before we get further into curation, you want to forget your passwords.

FORGET YOUR PASSWORDS

Once we have the three identities on your computer with a clear split in purpose, we want to make sure they stay that way.

Most web-based applications are accessible from the browser. Keeping these environments separate can be really hard, because we can simply log in to Twitter or Facebook from the browser in the Create or Communicate mode. There is one simple trick with identity management to increase friction towards our worst tendencies. The best part is that this also makes our online experience safer. This trick is to use a password manager to manage your identities.

Password managers remember passwords, which means that we can forget them.

Let's say you find yourself logging in to Twitter when you're supposed to be responding to emails. First, log in to the Curate mode and go to the offending website. Use the reset password option. When prompted for a new password, use your password manager to randomly generate a really long password, which would be impossible to remember. For example, below is a randomly generated thirty-character password, which should be quite a headache to recall and type:

vqk3@gs3FNHA5HRV4r$ku7X*MNYyuc

Make sure that this password is only stored in the password manager in your Curate mode. If you don't remember the password, you simply won't be able to access your Twitter feed from anywhere else. You should also make sure that the password to your website blocker app is also only available from the Curate mode. This way you won't be able to fiddle with the blocking settings from inside the Create or Communicate mode.

You can apply this approach to the passwords of the three user accounts themselves. You can choose shorter passwords for your Create and Communicate accounts and a longer password for your Curate account. You may even choose a password that will remind you of your priorities. For example, you can set your password to 'Have I spent time with family?'

If you're on a deadline and trying to stop yourself from accessing all distractions, you can change the password to your Curate account to a random, long string. Write down this random password carefully on a piece of paper, and seal it. This password is the master key to all your distractions. Depending on your ability to self-regulate, you can either hide it or leave it with a trusted friend. You can even ask your friend to not give it back to you till you prove you are done with the work you were supposed to finish.

Bear in mind, however, that the objective isn't to avoid spending any time in the Curate mode. If anything, this is probably where you will have your best ideas. If used well, you can learn a lot from the internet and meet interesting people too. But like with focused work or efficient communication, it needs to be done mindfully.

Let's understand how we can do this.

CURATE WITH CONTEXT

The way we usually lose time to content is when we try and sneak in just a quick look, but go down a spiral. To avoid this, many of us open tabs, or email/text ourselves links, with the intent of reading them later.

Most of us will never get around to these.

Yet, these unopened tabs and links sit there, demanding our attention, adding to the list of 'open loops' that do not help us in keeping our mind clear. With open tabs, one can actually feel the open loops weighing down on the extended mind, as it slows down one's computer.

There already are popular apps designed to help with this tendency. Pocket, Readwise and Instapaper are the most popular ones. These allow you to add links from anywhere with just one press of a button. When you have the time, you can read/watch all the links you've saved for later. Separating curation from consumption is, generally speaking, a good idea.

But most users of these apps with whom we spoke told us that they never really go through or finish what is in the app. The problem is the act of browsing through our feeds and saving a link for later is more instantly gratifying than the act of actually going through the backlog and reading it. Even when we do try to go back, we find it hard to recall why this particular link was of interest to us.

Instead of using any of the apps, we recommend using your working memory to make your own Read Later list. Whenever you come across a link you want to read later, or if your friend recommended a link to you, save it to your working memory.

The only difference is that we want to slightly increase the friction of saving a link, so that we don't create a huge backlog for ourselves. Instead of only saving the link, write a sentence or two about the context in which you came across the link and why you want your future self to read it. For example, *'#Recommended by Priyanka. this (link) #podcast discussing the new book by Michael Lewis. She told me it has good writing advice and also recommendations for good reads by Lewis. Leisure Listen. #ReadLater'*

Add a standardized tag such as #ReadLater. If it was recommended to you, mention that too and mention who recommended it. Use tags or other details to classify the link by either category, project or priority. Make the system as personal as you want.

Next time you have only a few minutes, try and view an item from your Read Later list in your working memory rather than browsing a new feed. The advantage of this list is that it is truly a personalized, highly curated list made by someone who knows your preferences and desires intimately—you. If done with patience, it would even include helpful commentary on why you should pick them. There is no feed in the world that will match your tastes better than the content in here.

Once you finish an item, move it out of the list or at least delete the tag that marked it as saved for later. You can go back and add some feedback to the list after you've read the article. Another advantage of separating curation and adding feedback is that over time, you will be able to see the quality of recommendations from each of your sources. You will start getting a sense of the people and publications that send you good content versus those that do not.

This method hopefully adds enough friction to slow down the open tab backlog, but it won't eliminate it. For that, we have to use the Nuclear Option.

THE NUCLEAR OPTION

One of the reasons we hoard content to consume is because we overestimate the time and energy our future selves will have. We keep adding things to our list, believing that someday we will find the magical, herculean energy required to go through everything.

To solve this, strictly implement the nuclear option.

Every week at a fixed time, you must delete all items from your Read Later list, whether you've read them or not. If you have some programming skills, you can even set up your computer to do this automatically. This deletion part of the curation process is the most important. If you don't do this, there is no incentive for you to actually consume the content you've curated. Or maybe the content you saved was not good enough.

Either way, it is a new week, and you start with a clean slate. Try to do better this time.

The more strictly this rule is implemented, the more real the stakes become. As the deadline gets closer, you start looking at the content you've saved with very different eyes. You start prioritizing items with value and discard those not worth your time. The time that has passed between when you saved and when you consume helps you re-evaluate whether it is still relevant. The context that you've saved along with the item helps with this task immensely.

If you flush a bunch of saved links often, it will start changing your patterns of curation. You'll start saving less or adding better context. The feedback from this process will start helping you adjust what content you see and when. For many, the nuclear option will seem too harsh. People who think this are exactly those who need it. This is why it is called the nuclear option.

It is okay if you want to save a copy of this list for that rare future occurrence when you want to find a specific link you had once come across. As long as you are not treating the archives as an *active* list, saving is fine. The idea is to make the stakes real and to clear our minds of open loops. Personally, Tanuj saves all recommendations from people permanently in his working memory but only deletes the #ReadLater tag.

All of this is only useful if we consume with intent.

CONSUME WITH INTENT

If the objective is feeling calm and in control over our information diet, curation is insufficient; we also need to change the way we engage with content.

The overload of content makes us want to spend less time on each piece of content, not more. We learn how to skim and speed-read. Next to every interesting talk or video are recommendations for five more that seem equally, if not more, interesting. We listen to podcasts and videos on 2× to blaze through the ideas. Often, we go through these feeds and links without really engaging with the ideas or thoughts within.

This approach may help us plough through more content, but are we getting value from it?

We will forget an overwhelming majority of what we read, watch or listen. The less time we spend on something, the less likely it is that we will remember the ideas in it. For any idea to have an effect, you need to be able to give it deliberate attention. You need to be able to think about the ideas for at least some time.

Thankfully, we are already aware of a way to give our focused attention to an idea. It is to use our working memory to take notes. Every time you're reading or watching something, open up your working memory and make some notes about what you just saw. Slow down to put the idea in your own words. Make connections with ideas and thoughts you've had previously.

As Feynman and Buffet did, try to explain the idea in clear terms to your future self to help you think better now. The pleasant side-effect is that you also create a record of your own thinking. Your future self will thank you. If you forget the ideas you had, your notes will explain them to you.

When you make taking notes the objective of your consumption, the process of consumption goes from passive to active. Your mind finds it easier to focus. You gain a sharper eye for what is and isn't good content. You learn to skip over content that has nothing new for you. Over time, you'll be able to start ignoring entire feeds that no longer teach you anything new.

Active consumption doesn't increase the amount of content you consume. Nor does it increase the relevance of the sources you've picked. What it does is ensure that the time you spend on a piece of content is meaningful. Your notes become the tangible outcome of what you've learnt.

Furthermore, you end up collecting all the ideas you learn in your working memory. This alone is a huge benefit. You will be able to see connections between ideas you've had years apart. These connections will help you have original ideas, since the specific universe of content you've seen is as unique as your fingerprint.

Instead of going through most content, you engage deeply with curated content. You start seeing exponential growth in your own knowledge and creativity.

NURTURE YOUR CREATIVE SELF

During the pandemic, many of us had more than usual idle time.

Quite a few of us started filling up the time with more consumption on the internet and, in general, spending more time collectively on social media. People could identify that this was a drain on them emotionally. This draining but compulsive act came to be known as 'doomscrolling'.

The problem with attention economy companies is that they are trying to take over every second of our idle time. They want to replace it with more and more content consumption. The CEO of Netflix once said that one of Netflix's competitors is sleep. People are staying up late to watch shows, so that's where he expects the increased watch time metrics to come from. 'And we're winning!', he added.

When we have time to spare, the choice of simply passively consuming a video or scrolling through a feed is much easier. We understand that overconsumption is harmful. But it is incredibly hard to stop. All the strategies we present in this book will help, but we're aware that they aren't bulletproof.

The only sure-shot way to streamline your consumption is to nurture your creativity.

Even when we curate well, consume actively, and use the Nuclear Option to clear the consumption backlogs, we're still only consuming. Humans have an innate desire to express themselves. Whether it is fashion, writing, making videos, jokes, poetry, drawing, sculpting or anything else, we're significantly more engaged and fulfilled when we're making art and expressing our identities. We don't even need much of an audience; the act of expressing itself is enough.

You can change the internet from a source of distraction into an outlet for your creativity. Sharing on the internet is wonderful because there's an audience for everyone. You don't need to be world-class to be sharing on the internet. If what you make helps even one person, then the two of you are better off for it. The feedback you get from sharing can be invigorating and make you want to get better at your art.

Creativity also requires us to value our idle time. Being creative is about seeing connections between seemingly unrelated things. This is impossible if you are always being productive. We don't believe that there is a hierarchy amongst the modes we've created. The aim isn't to spend as little time in the Curate mode; it is to be fully immersed in whatever mode you need to be.

Dr Barbara Oakley, a professor of engineering at Oakland University, is the creator of the incredibly popular online course 'Learning to Learn'. In her journal article titled 'The Middle Way: Finding the Balance between Mindfulness and Mind-Wandering', she claims that both focused and diffused attention are essential to learning. We absorb information in focused mode, but in diffused mode, our brains make connections between them. This is why so many of us have novel ideas that just 'came to us' when we were in the shower, driving or walking in the park.

Creativity requires balancing consumption with creation. You need to consume and create in cycles, just like you need to breathe in and breathe out. When you have creative projects, they tend to dictate the shape of what you consume to learn. What you consume inspires and shapes what you create.

The problem is that instead of being our creative selves, many of us have become the ideal consumers of the attention economy. We're willing to forgo all our idle time, even our sleep, so that these companies can keep growing. This was never the original purpose or the plan for the internet. The internet was meant to connect us so that we could share ideas, not passively consume content.

If you want to change your relationship with technology, you're going to have to change the idea of yourself from being a passive consumer to being an active creator. Your extended mind isn't just a way for you to get information or content from others. It is a way for you to put your own content out there, adding to the collective experience.

To really get the most out of the internet, you need to put your *selves* out there.

11

HOW TO BE LEFT ALONE

OUR SELVES

Before the COVID-19 pandemic threatened our lives, an increasing number of researchers had begun to identify a new epidemic. Just like we discovered that obesity is linked to heart disease or smoking is linked to cancer, this lifestyle has been linked to various physical and mental health issues. Douglas Nemecek, chief medical officer for behavioural health at the large insurance firm Cigna, said that this new epidemic 'has the same impact on mortality as smoking 15 cigarettes a day, making it even more dangerous than obesity'. What is this silent killer?

Loneliness.

Scientists have proven that isolation can have various detrimental effects, not just on humans, but on many social animals. Isolation increases the levels of cortisol, the stress hormone, in pigs and monkeys, just as it does in humans. Fruit flies have reduced lifespans when isolated. Rats are more at risk of obesity and Type II diabetes when isolated. It isn't surprising that loneliness is deadly in humans too. Group foraging and hunting may have been critical for human survival thousands of years ago, but they seem much less important in today's modern economy. Then why does loneliness persist?

Humans are social animals. Our ability to cooperate was selected by evolution because it helped us thrive. The pain of loneliness made us socialize, just like hunger makes us eat or feeling cold makes us seek shelter. Even the language we use for social failures—'She broke my heart', 'He hurt her feelings', 'I was burning with shame'—speak of it as if it is literal pain. We've managed to overcome our primitive lifestyles, but the social instincts that made us who we are still persist. It is in our very nature to care about our relationships and our social standing. All humans have a deep need for connection and belonging. We find it hard to be ourselves, without also belonging to something larger than our selves.

Loneliness may be a killer, but that also doesn't mean that we're designed to be with everyone all the time. We need and enjoy solitude just as much as we need and enjoy company. Sometimes, we just want to be left alone or be wholly interested in our own pursuits. We want space from others so that we can relax and be who we truly are. We may have thoughts and feelings that we do not want to share with others. Sometimes privacy is a need that arises precisely because we care so much about our social standing. We have secrets, often embarrassing, that we do not want widely known because we care about what people think about us.

As humans, all of us have had to learn to walk the fine line between figuring out who we truly are, while also managing what others think we are—a balancing act between our desire for socializing and our desire for privacy.

In the digital age, this fine line has become vanishingly thin. We leave digital breadcrumbs wherever we go, revealing things about ourselves to corporations and prying governments we don't even tell our closest friends. Moreover, a lot of our social interactions have shifted online, and social media has become the place where we go to fulfil our desire for connection and belonging. Social media has become critical to our lives, but does it really give us the social connections and sense of belonging we seek? If not, then why do so many people spend so much time there?

In this chapter and the next, we try to develop a *bitful* approach to both these competing desires. In this chapter, we cover how to keep to your self, i.e., how to reclaim your privacy. In the next chapter, we cover strategies for how we can use our technology more mindfully when connecting with others online.

Let us start by learning how to be left alone.

PRIVACY IS BOUNDARY MANAGEMENT

Privacy is a big problem on the internet.

Nearly all online activities generate a trail of data. Someone or the other always knows what you're doing in every moment of time. For every commercial transaction, at the very least, your payments provider will have a record. For every website you visit, your internet service provider will know where you've been. If you spend time on any website with ads, many third-party data brokers and other ad-tech firms will know that you visited. Each of these intermediaries has a portion of your data and is in the market either selling what they have or buying more of it.

It is impossible to prevent this data generation in the first place. Ideally companies should only record data that is necessary to deliver a service. The data should only be used in ways aligned with our interests, such as to improve the product or to troubleshoot a bug. In reality, companies collect a lot more data because it is cheap as well as lucrative to do so. For one reason or another, our data ends up in a server somewhere. What we should be concerned about is what happens next.

A lot of this data is up for sale. Some of it directly in targeted advertising markets. The games you install may sell your location data to marketers. Sometimes if the data is not up for sale, the company itself could be. In 2016, the Beijing-based Kunlun group acquired the US-based gay dating app, Grindr. The Committee of Foreign Investments in the United States (CFIUS) soon sought to reverse this deal, citing national security concerns. Grindr had data about the sexuality, HIV status, and private messages of more than 27 million Americans. Due to CFIUS' intervention, the company was eventually acquired by a set of US-based investors.

Generation of data is inevitable, but its use for surveillance is not. In a mostly online world, privacy is not the same as anonymity.

Privacy is boundary management.

Privacy means being able to assert control over who has access to what data about us. It means being able to express who *doesn't* have access or what they *can't* use it for and knowing that our wishes will be respected.

PRIVACY IS BOUNDARY MANAGEMENT

Privacy is not locking up your data
so no one can see

Privacy is being able to control
who sees what about you

The fundamental tool that we will use is the same as the previous section—our identity. The previous section used identity to help create a boundary between goal-oriented use of our devices from other general-purpose or leisure use. In this section, we want to see how well-defined identities can help us create boundaries around our data and ourselves to help us reclaim a sense of privacy.

PRIVACY IN PRACTICE

Many companies now market privacy as a feature. This leads many to believe that privacy is simply a binary, either something has privacy or it doesn't. In practice, depending on what measures you have taken, you will have a *degree* of privacy.

Configuring for privacy almost always involves some trade-offs. At the very least, you'll need to put in a little bit of time to configure your devices and learn the habits you need to maintain your desired level of privacy. To do this optimally without feeling overwhelmed, one first needs to answer—what is my desired level of privacy? and what am I willing to do to meet it?

To be able to answer what your desired level of privacy is, you must be aware of what you are protecting and from whom. For some people, merely the idea of being tracked makes them shudder.

It makes them willing to invest in any measure to protect themselves. For some, browsing history being tracked for ads does not seem creepy, but privacy to them may mean the right to not be bombarded with spam emails or incessant marketing calls.

Most of our privacy is not lost to clever hackers; instead, we lose it through oversharing. The companies that benefit from advertising are also the ones in charge of configuring our privacy preferences. By default, these preferences favour their business model over the individual. If you really want to protect your privacy, you will need to put in the effort to change settings and learn new behaviours.

Once you understand the risks and your own preferences, you need to design a plan for yourself that you can implement easily. We list some strategies below that might help you decide what you are willing to realistically protect.

First, you need to be practical. It is more likely that you will abandon an ill-designed plan that was too ambitious. A simpler plan that protects your basics without much effort might serve you better in the long run.

We recommend that, at a bare minimum, everyone must learn what it takes to protect:

- **Identity Credentials:** Passwords to emails or social media accounts that may be used to impersonate you. Any identifiers such as national identity numbers, drivers license numbers, etc., which are meant to be secret, should be protected too.
- **Financial Information:** Banking details and details of credit cards, etc. These are the most common targets of all cybercrime.

Communication: Being able to have completely private conversations.
- **Location and Addresses:** Whether GPS coordinates or physical addresses to prevent you from being physically tracked or harmed.
- **Other Personally Identifying Information or Sensitive Data:** Any other data or documents that you'd rather not be in the public sphere such as your browsing history, your journal or other personal documents.

It is also important to understand what you cannot control. Every time you use an online service for a transaction—to order food, do shopping, call a taxi, book a hotel, etc.—you will generate a log on their server, and possibly with some intermediaries such as your payments provider. These companies and intermediaries will retain this information for as long as their privacy policy states. These companies may then sell this data or hand it to the government if requested, as per their policies and the laws of the land. This is not something you can individually change, but you can be mindful of when deciding your desired privacy level.

Since these individual transactions happen on different websites, once again it is your identity that helps them connect these pieces together and create a deep profile of you. If you are concerned about details from various aspects of your life being associated, do pay attention to which identifiers (emails, phone numbers, etc.) you are revealing to them.

Ultimately, there is no magic bullet solution to privacy on the internet. There are only measures you can take to be a harder target to trace. In the sections that follow, we'll be going over how to attain specific types of privacy.

PHRASES NOT WORDS

In October of 2020, Donald Trump's Twitter account was allegedly hacked by a Dutch researcher. He had access to the account of the then President of the United States and could read his direct messages. There was no elaborate code or trick. He simply guessed the password and apparently got it on his fifth try. The researcher claims Trump's password was 'maga2020!'

We're often told that we should make our passwords difficult to guess by adding special characters or numbers, but this is bad advice. The creator of this 2003 standard, Bill Burr, has admitted he regrets having written the document. When humans try to follow this best practice, they come up with very predictable passwords. Replacing 'a' with @, adding exclamations at the end of passwords, using anniversaries and birthdays for random numbers, etc.

Worst of all, this makes passwords harder to remember for humans. We end up using the same password in multiple places. This is terrible for security. The password to your bank account is now only as safe as the security protections on the weakest website where you reused the password. A simple phishing attack, that is, someone making a fake website asking you to login, would be enough for you to lose access to most of your accounts.

Most hackers who would simply guess would try to use computers to guess. For a computer, guessing 'maga2020!' is the same as guessing 'dfaa9183@'. The most important criterion isn't variability of characters, it is the length of the password. The longer your password, the more guesses a computer has to make. This means that instead of a pass*word*, you might be better off thinking of a pass*phrase*. The longer the phrase, the better.

The other way hackers attack is password reuse. If you use the same password everywhere, the security of your bank account is only as much as the security of neopets.com. Hackers simply guess passwords you've used on other sites to get into more sensitive apps or websites.

Ideally, you should have different passwords for each website. This will prevent password reuse attacks, but it leads to using a lot of passwords. You can use a password manager to store all your passwords. Password managers help you generate random, long passwords that are hard to guess. It then fills in these passwords automatically when you are browsing, if you have logged into the password manager. This means that you don't reuse passwords on any site, but still only have to remember one master password.

Most password managers also allow you to save other secrets such as your banking details, credit card numbers, ID numbers, software license keys, etc., in an encrypted manner. The advantage is that all your secrets are safely stored as encrypted files rather than plain text. They are in one convenient location and can even be autofilled directly where you need them. The trade-off is that there is now a single point of failure. But you can offset some of that risk by using two-factor authentication (2FA) on your password manager.

A second factor of authentication is basically an additional way of confirming that you are really you. Ideally, your password is a secret that only you know. However, in case your password has leaked, the 2FA confirms your identity by sending a one-time password to a device that is known to be in your control.

In fact, as far as possible, you should be using 2FA on all your important accounts, especially your financial accounts. There are multiple choices for second factors as well, and they have their own trade-offs between security, convenience and costs. If you can afford it, try to get a physical security key based on an open standard such as U2F to act as your second factor.

PRIVACY FROM BEING ANNOYED

When we imagine our privacy being lost, we imagine a motivated stalker or a determined enemy is trying to ascertain what we're doing, whom we're meeting and what we're saying in an attempt to harm or harass us. This happens to a lot of people, especially women. For men and women alike, it is much more likely that they face the less dangerous, more common, but still annoying problem of being bombarded by an incessant stream of marketing calls, messages and emails.

Many businesses, online or offline, ask us for our number or email to transact with them. Some residential as well as office buildings also ask for these details to permit entry into them. This data then makes its way, either directly sold by the company or indirectly by an unscrupulous agent, to a marketing database. From there, it is sold repeatedly to anyone who wants it. Even if the company has a privacy policy, if they don't implement security well, this data can leak. Now you have a spam problem and your details are also easily available to any motivated attacker or stalker.

Whether stalking, surveillance or spam, the underlying problem is the same.

Our communication channels are architected to be open to anyone who has our unique identifier. That is, anyone with our email address can email us and anyone with our phone number can call us.

The architecture favours the harassers. Even though regulators such as the Telecom Regulatory Authority of India (TRAI) have instated penalties and a National Do Not Call registry, enforcement is hard. For a motivated spammer or stalker, the costs of getting a new number or a new email are very low. Neither we nor the regulator can humanly keep up with the task of blocking each new number or email ID that they get. On the other hand, the personal cost and inconvenience of changing our number, resending it to all our family, friends and acquaintances is high.

We can protect our privacy from such annoyances by splitting our identity.

Emails and phone numbers usually act as our primary identifier across SMS as well as chat apps such as WhatsApp, Telegram and Signal. Managing email ids and phone numbers is, thus, a good bottleneck to manage privacy preferences across all of these applications and channels.

Just like we split our personality on our devices by the quality of attention, we should split our communication channels by the level of privacy we desire. Just like we talked about three kinds of information environments, consider the following levels of privacy.

1. **Trusted Contacts:** This includes friends, family and others who should be able to reach you whenever they desire.
2. **Utility Contacts:** This includes services like a plumber or a delivery person whom you share contact details with for a specific utility. During a specific context or time period, you want them to be able to reach you, but not otherwise.
3. **Burner Contacts:** These are places that force you to hand over your email or phone number. You don't really want to hear from them, but it is the price of admission. You may want to share an identifier to gain a one-time entry, but you don't care at all about hearing from them again.

The internet makes creating new email ids very easy. The appendix lists some places where you can create burner email ids for temporary use. The most common use of temporary email ids is to get to content on sites that force you to register and then later bombard you with emails. Burner email ids are completely air-gapped from your real one, so you don't have to worry about future spam.

Today, there are services available that let you make virtual numbers as well. Virtual numbers are numbers different from your main number and can be operated through apps. They can be set up to receive calls and SMSes without requiring an additional subscriber identity module (SIM). Calls from unknown numbers can be automatically blocked, while those from trusted numbers can be redirected. These numbers can also be used to register and create a secondary account on services like WhatsApp, Telegram or Signal.

We can use different identities for different levels of privacy. Setting up a new email or virtual number should take you ten minutes at most. Once you do, you now have an air-gapped email or phone number, which you can use as a utility or burner and share without fear.

Instead of using your real name, number or email, consider creating a completely unique, unrelated identity for e-commerce deliveries. This way even if the address leaks, they are not linked to your real-world identity.

It is helpful in general to use a burner email to subscribe to new, unimportant services. This has multiple advantages. First, the email ID that makes it to most databases is not the primary email you use for services such as banking or for private correspondence. As we discussed in Chapter 10, you can even use another email ID for collecting newsletters. Separating newsletters into another ID means your personal inbox is not filled with newsletters, promotional emails or spam, drastically cutting down the volume of email you have to deal with.

It may seem like a task to juggle multiple identities, but most of it becomes automatic if you're using a password manager. Password managers don't just remember your passwords, they remember usernames too. When you visit any website or app, they let you simply pick from all the identities you have registered on that website.

Even important services require you to register using an email address, and some of them don't respect your privacy from being annoyed. You can set up a dedicated email ID only to sign up for these services. This way, all the unnecessary notification emails do not crowd your primary inbox, protecting not just your privacy but also your attention.

PRIVACY OF YOUR CONVERSATIONS:
END-TO-END ENCRYPTION

We don't need to spend any time explaining why the secrecy of our private communications is very important. Only when our conversations are secure, can we feel free to say what we need to. We want to focus on how our conversations can leak and what we should do to prevent it.

There are essentially three ways in which our conversations can become public:

1. In transit by intermediaries
2. Through compromised personal devices
3. Intentional or unintentional disclosure by the receiver of communications

The first scenario is when the people responsible for delivering your messages can read them. Lately, end-to-end encryption has become widely available on our instant messaging apps. Due to their design, SMSes should be considered not private for all practical purposes. You may want to look for an end-to-end encrypted email service as well. See the Appendix for a complete list of services.

Even if your communication channel is end-to-end encrypted, the ends themselves can still leak. It is alleged that the assassination of journalist Jamaal Khashoggi was coordinated with the help of information obtained from leaked WhatsApp conversations with another Saudi dissident, Omar Abdulaziz. Abdulaziz's phone had spyware delivered by a masked link, masquerading as a tracking link for a package. There is little one can do if the devices themselves have been compromised by motivated attackers. If you're really in need of strong privacy, you have to make sure that both you and your conversation partner are using a secure device.

All of us may not have to worry about protection from heavily resourced state intelligence apparatus. However, there is no saying which of the conversations we had today will leak in the future and create a problem for us. The problem with maintaining privacy is that it is not a bounded problem. An end-to-end secure chat between you and a loved one today may end up being compromised in 5 years' time due to a malicious app that your child accidentally downloaded while playing a game.

Our best hedge against this unbounded risk is to choose ephemerality.

FORGETTING AND FORGIVING

Since computer storage is cheap, many providers default to saving all your messages and posts. This seems like a great idea because you can go back and search for every message that someone has sent you. However, when you think about privacy, it is worth asking if every message is really worth saving.

As a society, we underappreciate the value of forgetting. It is not just privacy, it is about our emotional well-being.

Since we're used to looking up old links, or jokes or memes that our friends sent, we have started believing that having all messages stored forever is a good thing. However, just because some messages are useful to look up later, doesn't mean saving all messages is beneficial.

We've all said things when we're hurt or angry, in person, on text or on social media, that we regret. There are also things posted that simply fall out of favour or become inappropriate with the passage of time. In person, we forget most of our conversations. If someone said something hurtful, we eventually even forgive them. In digital mediums, such messages remain on record forever. Whether they are on the sending or receiving end of regrettable messages, some people tend to go back and ruminate on these unhealthily.

Many instant messages now allow you the option to make your messages ephemeral. That is, they disappear after a certain period of time. Some services allow you to even set the time period of this disappearance. We recommend you use this feature extensively on your most personal relationships, especially with your spouse or partner. By default, the messages you sent each other will disappear.

This doesn't mean you can't save messages. Services that provide ephemerality also usually provide a method to save important messages, such as starring or forwarding. It increases the friction of saving a message. This small speed bump allows us to be more mindful about what we save. Instead of saving all the hurtful messages, we can ensure that our chat history only contains delightful memories. Opening the chat history presents you with these memories rather than the more mundane everyday stuff. Besides, you don't have to use these ephemeral messages with everyone, only for truly personal or sensitive conversations.

Ephemerality is not foolproof: anyone can still screenshot or save the messages you sent. It is only protection against the unknown unknown. It reduces the chances that sensitive information or pictures about you got leaked because, say, your friend's phone got stolen or someone forced their way into your phone. You don't have to turn on the feature with everyone. For example, with clients or work colleagues, it may be useful to have a history of conversations. These conversations usually also pose less of a privacy risk.

Where you use ephemerality and where you don't is a boundary you need to set, based on your personal expectation of privacy.

PRIVACY FROM TRACKING

The strongest argument to prevent tracking is the asymmetry of risk and reward. There is generally very little for you to gain from targeted advertising or other surveillance, but the potential harms of a motivated attacker having access to your entire browsing history could be huge.

You should adopt as many of these measures as you comfortably can based on your assessment of your privacy risks.

PROTECTION FROM THE UNKNOWN UNKNOWN

Sometimes you might need to be extra sure that there is no trace of what you're doing. You may find it useful to use Tor Browser.

Tor is short for The Onion Router. The internet is basically one large open network. You can use encryption such that only the intended recipient will be able to read the contents of your request. However, the meta-data, i.e., the data about who sent the request, when and to whom is sent openly. Think about the postman and the envelope. The envelope protects the contents of the message, but what's on the address is public, so that the postman can deliver the message to the right address. There is a certain degree of privacy loss if someone can read the addresses you communicate with, even if they can't read what you're communicating about.

Instead of taking the shortest route, the Tor browser routes every request through multiple, random servers. At each hop, information is masked, and a layer of encryption is added (hence, the 'onion' router). Even if a hop is compromised, it could, at best, only know the addresses of one hop ahead and one hop behind. Because of the layers of encryption, no hop individually can decrypt the information. At no point in the journey does any one computer know both the original sender and the receiver, offering a truly anonymous browsing session.

Tor is the safest browser, but also the slowest. Tor's multiple hops make page loading slower. An alternative strategy is to simply protect yourself from tracking at two levels. First, protection from the ISPs who track you using the hardware they provide to connect to the internet. Second, protection from advertisers who track you using browsers, apps and other software you use to use the internet.

PROTECTION FROM YOUR ISP

Your ISP is the bottleneck to all your internet usage. All requests from all your devices pass through them. They know what all the members of your family are up to. You can do two things to make sure you're safe.

1. **Use HTTPS everywhere:** The original protocol of the internet didn't really have security in mind. All your data was transmitted in plain text and could be read by anyone in the middle. Using HTTPS prevents them from being able to read the contents of the websites you are accessing. Using https is as simple as making sure the uniform resource locator (URL) you are currently on begins with 'https://'. Most browsers also have a visual indicator to show that you are using https. Usually this looks like a green lock.
2. **Use a paid, secure, non-logging VPN:** Anytime you visit a website or access an app, all ISPs can see the internet address

of the destination, even if you're using HTTPS. Virtual Private Networks (VPNs) route your traffic through their own private servers. The ISPs can now see the address of the VPN but will not know your final destination.

Beware that there are many 'free' VPNs that may protect your data from your ISP but may instead sell it themselves or make available your history on request. If you really want to be private, opt for a paid VPN that does not log traffic.

3. **Ensure that your DNS is private too:** The way the internet is architected is that internet addresses are pure numbers called IP Addresses, for example, 123.45.67.89. However, since humans are bad at remembering these numbers, we created domain names such as google.com, apple.com, and so many more. A domain name server (DNS) translates between human-readable addresses and IP addresses. Every time you click a link or type in a URL, your request is first sent to a DNS, which translates that URL into an IP address. This is another potential source of leakage, even if you do use VPNs. The Appendix lists open DNSes and how to change them.

PROTECTION FROM THE ADVERTISERS

The other entities likely to track all your browsing history are the adtech companies. The very first thing to remember is that they use your identity to recognize you. Due to rising awareness of the extent of data collection, many of these companies have started offering privacy choices.

MANAGING IDENTITY

The primary way that ad networks track you is because you've logged into their products. For browsing that you do not want to be linked to your identity, you can use the incognito mode. Or even install a different browser if that works better for you. If you do install another browser, remember to never login to your existing social media or email accounts, else advertising companies will be able to set a cookie knowing that you are you. If you've already split by identity, you can set up your browsers in each personality for the level of privacy you desire.

CHANGE YOUR DEFAULTS

There are a few steps you can take to prevent adtech networks from creating profiles of you. You can also stop re-targeting ads which will no longer try and tempt you with things you almost purchased. The following checklist summarizes the steps you can take to prevent your data being collected at all. Some specific sites may not function correctly because of some of these, but those should be the exceptions, not the rule.

- Opt out of all participating ad networks on youradchoices.com
- Opt out of ad personalization and data sharing from Google and Facebook
- Change your default search engine to something that does not save your history
- Change your browser to a more private one such as Brave or Firefox.
- Change your current browser's settings to 'do not track' and block third-party cookies
- You can use different identities on your browser to prevent linking of browsing history and targeting of ads.
- If your browser supports it, get privacy-protecting extensions from the Electronic Frontier Foundation (EFF) such as privacy badger, HTTPS everywhere, etc.
- Reset advertising IDs on your smartphone as often as you can

A recently updated detailed how-to of each of these steps is available at bitfulness.com/privacy.

PRIVACY ON SOCIAL MEDIA

Social media poses a much more challenging problem to privacy than any other kind of app or website. The strategies outlined in this chapter focus on preventing inadvertent sharing of personal data and identifiers that could result in harm if shared outside of trusted circles. We do this by protecting our real identity from those who would track us.

On the other hand, you go to social media precisely to share personal information or, at the very least, information relevant to you personally. Everything you see, post or do on social media reflects *who you are*. You are revealing your self to the world, and the world is welcome to react to it directly.

The other challenge of social media is that we need to not just regulate the bits we exhale, we also need to regulate the bits we inhale. What we subscribe to, what we share, what we like is also causing changes to what our news feeds show. There's a feedback loop at work here that is opaque to us. However, this feedback loop determines our news feed. Through our feed, it affects our world view, our social circle and even our peace of mind.

To understand how we can have a *bitful* approach to social media, we need to first understand what social media really does.

12

HOW TO BE TOGETHER

THE DRESS

In 2015, Cecilia Bleasdale used her phone to take a picture of a dress at Cheshire Oaks Designer Outlet north of Chester, England. Bleasdale planned on wearing this dress to her daughter's wedding and sent her daughter the picture to get her opinion. Her daughter would eventually post the photo to Facebook to ask her friends a simple question:

What colour was The Dress?

The picture Bleasdale's daughter posted is the famous meme that divided the planet on whether The Dress is black and blue or gold and white. It originated on Facebook but went viral across all social media networks. Major television and print news outlets covered the story. Fans wanted to know whether celebrities saw blue or gold. News items about The Dress itself went viral. Wired Magazine's article by Adam Rogers on The Dress got over 32.8 million unique visitors. The hashtag '#TheDress' was generating more than 11,000 tweets a minute. At one point, there were more than 8,40,000 views a minute of the Tumblr post. Buzzfeed's poll on The Dress broke its then-record for most concurrent users live on the site.

The Dress exemplifies how social media really works.

If you are curious to know, The Dress was black and blue, but more than two thirds who saw the picture saw it as white and gold.

There is no scientific consensus as to why people saw discordant colours. But The Dress went viral precisely because it divided opinion in a manner that can't be settled definitively. In a rare instance, The Dress was one of the things that divided us but was also incredibly low stakes. You could disagree with someone but also laugh about it together. Usually, for more high-stakes questions such as politics, policy, gender, justice or even sports, the conversations can get acrimonious rather quickly. The resulting hate attracts even more people into the brawl and drives more engagement.

Social media has its upsides too. For example, in the second wave of the COVID-19 pandemic in 2021, Twitter users in India self-organized to move huge amounts of relief in the form of oxygen cylinders, medicines, plasma and other materials. Cryptocurrency founders put together a relief fund for India that received nearly US$400 million in relief funds from across the globe. Although the verdict is still out, it is a group of Twitter users who incessantly researched and collaborated to put the lab leak hypothesis back on the table. Social media is undeniably interesting and covers niches you wouldn't even dream existed. You can genuinely build connections with people across the globe, or across the room, in a new and different way. There have been real social movements that have been born and grown on social media.

Social media has become an inextricable part of society. Whether you individually decide to opt-in or opt-out of social media, it still deeply affects your life anyway. Hence, it deserves much more of our scrutiny.

People are often worried, and rightfully so, about *What is social media doing to society?* Or, at a more personal level, *What is social media doing to my data?*

We believe we need to start with a more basic question—*What is social media?*

WHAT IS SOCIAL MEDIA?

Social media is both a slice of public opinion and the thing that shapes it.

Social media posts don't always come with the right (or even *any*) facts, but it always carries the point of view of those who post them.

This is both its appeal and its curse. Scientists set up an experiment where they took a set of photos and displayed it in an Instagram-style feed to subjects under a functional magnetic resonance imaging (an fMRI) machine. They experimented with the feed, showing the same photos to everyone, but a different number of likes. The brain scans showed that subjects consistently paid more attention to the photos with more likes. It didn't matter if the photos were the ones they posted or the ones they saw. The results revealed a simple truth.

We pay a *lot* more attention to information others value.

On social media, we don't just learn about what is happening in the world, we learn a thing that's even more important—what others in our networks *have to say* about what is happening in the world. The beliefs we adopt are not formed independently, we adopt beliefs that serve us socially. Influencers exist because we're surprisingly easily influenced. We make complex judgements such as which brands we trust, where to take our next vacations or whom we will vote for, based on what others say on social media. Even if we aren't conscious of doing so.

In turn, this is also social media's curse. We use people to value information, but we also use information to value people. We tend to agree with things said by people we like and disagree with those we don't, even if we don't do that consciously. We tend to share articles that confirm our world-views, and we look at how much an article is shared by our network as evidence of it being true. Fake news spreads far because we're not looking at the news, we're paying more attention to who shared it. Simultaneously, we call news shared by people we dislike, fake. Social media is where we express what we have to say about what is happening in our world and where others judge us on the basis of what we express.

This judgement can have terrible consequences for people and often arrives in full force and without warning. Once a group has judged someone or some institution worthy of scorn, extreme elements in an online tribe tend to harass and abuse their victims with impunity. While they may represent only a small fraction of their large community, for an individual on the receiving end, the absolute number of messages of hate, abuse, death or rape threats can be quite overwhelming.

Social media is really hard to quit. As social animals, information about what others are doing and what others think about us occupies a special place in our brains. Improving, or at the very least maintaining, our social standing occupies large parts of our attention. Social media plugs right into this primal desire.

This is why the *bitful* approach to social media isn't to stop or ignore it. Instead, it is to be a lot more intentional about what you want out of social media and configure your technology to make sure you get it. The exact recipe to do that will vary from person to person. However, the first step is the same for everyone, which is deciding what you *really* want from social media.

Is social media where you learn new things? Or is it where you catch up with friends? Maybe you use it to relax by switching off and watching mindless content. Don't judge your uses, just note them down before you get to the next section. Once you know what you want from social media, we dive deep into the strategies to get it in the next section.

A *BITFUL* LENS TO SOCIAL MEDIA

In theory, social media is our window to the world. In practice, social media is not a window but a *lens*.

When we look at the world through social media, we need to be more mindful that it is a *distorted* view of the world. You do have some autonomy over what you post and who is in your network, but largely the social network decides who sees what exactly. The algorithm we know selects content that *magnifies* differences.

Researchers at Facebook and Cornell proved the control your feed has over your emotions with a chilling experiment. They manipulated the content in the feed of over 7,00,000 users to either suppress or increase posts with emotional content. What they found was striking. First, emotions increase engagement. Remove all negative or positive emotions from a user's feed, and the user will post less. They also proved the existence of 'emotional contagion', i.e., when users were shown positive emotional content, their own posts were more positive and vice versa.

Social media companies control user feeds to run targeted advertising campaigns, which is how they earn. To maximize earning, they need to maximize engagement. They do this by algorithmically matching content to users. This matching of content to users is the fundamental dynamic at the heart of social media. Hence, you do not see the entirety of what the world sees; you only see that which the news feed algorithm chooses to show you to maximize engagement. Similarly, the algorithm decides the reach of your posts, thereby presenting a distorted image of you to the world. It sets you up for conflict, as your most provocative posts, even if they are comparatively rare, travel the furthest.

The end result is that everyone's a celebrity, everyone's a critic, and there's always conflict. Unless existing social media change drastically, getting the most out of them while protecting ourselves from harm is currently our own responsibility.

In practice, we tend to forget that social media is a distorting lens. We update our beliefs based on the world we see online and forget that it does not represent the real world but a specific collection of information deliberately selected to get a reaction out of us. The quickest way to get a sense of this is to swap phones with someone with reasonably different interests than you. Their social media news feed will look very different than yours.

Social media controls the fundamental dynamic, which means how our content is shared and displayed is not in our control, and neither are the posts we see. What is in our control are three dimensions—the identity we present, the content we share and our networks. These three levers of control allow us to push back against the distortion that social media pushes on us. Let us understand how we can put these into action.

SPECIALIZE

To design your own usage, you need to first answer: what do you use social media for? There are many uses and it would be impossible for us to list them all. But broadly, you can classify the uses into four categories—Connection, Fraternity, Community and Entertainment.

Connection represents our intimate relationships. People with whom we would like to share our personal joys, sorrows and everything else. Fraternity is those relationships where we share a common passion or interest. We want to share our knowledge, our questions and curiosities.

Community represents the roles we play as members of society. We want to present our best selves and participate in conversations about the future of our communities. Finally, entertainment is just that. It is leisure that doesn't require a reason.

Our simple strategy is to separate these four uses into four different social media networks or, at the very least, into four different accounts. Similar to how we split our personalities by attention mode in Chapter 7, we want to split our social media use by intent. The biggest upside is that it makes social media use much more intentional, with much less effort.

For example, if your friends are on Instagram, you can limit its use only to catch up with friends. Remove all content sources that are unrelated to your friends and family. You can use other networks such as Twitter, Reddit or Facebook to catch up on the news and explore your interests. Yes, this split adds friction, but that is the point. You want to be deliberate about which self you're being, rather than letting the social media algorithm decide your mood for you.

On a daily basis, instead of trying to limit your overall social media use, you can specifically limit use for Entertainment or Community or whatever you want to balance. It becomes easier to save your time and mental health, because you can block the specific social media app that is making you lose time or causing you distress. Connecting with friends on social media and seeing their happy moments is a true joy. Especially when in a world without social media, those moments may never have reached us at all. However, we start using social media with one intent, but often end up scrolling mindlessly till we're doing something else entirely.

Using social media to engage with our friends online has been shown to actually be positive for our well-being. Studies have shown that shallow engagements such as likes don't really make us feel connected online. When you see something that's interesting, try to leave a comment. If you'd rather talk to them one-on-one, even better!

In fact, if you truly want to use technology for connection, the best social network can be one you make. Let's call it a simple social to-do list. Write down a list of people you want to stay in touch with. Whenever you next have time, scroll till you find someone you haven't spoken to in a while. Drop them a message with a few updates about your life. Maybe mention a fond memory the two of you shared. Ask them when they're next available to talk over a phone or a video call. Once you've spoken to them, move them to the bottom of the list, so that your list always surfaces those whom you haven't spoken to in a while. Once a year or so, add or subtract names from the list to make sure it truly represents the people that matter to you. This simple list will help you create more meaningful connections than liking or sharing posts ever can.

CONTROL THE AUDIENCE

Social media's emphasis on follower counts and friend counts has led us all to add everyone to our one account, leading to the collapse of context. Today your best friend from college is as much as your 'friend' on Facebook, as Raj from accounting with whom you shared 6 sentences at the office party. Managing your privacy and preventing harm is harder if you use the same account for your inner and outer social circles.

If you do use social media to not just check but also to post updates, then the second dimension of control is very important. You should tightly control the audience of your Connection network to only your most trusted network and make your profile unsearchable. This allows you to be more vulnerable and share more intimate details with less fear of unintended consequences. This automatically improves your experience on social media, since you have a space where you can express yourself safely.

This is already how teenagers are using their social media. Many of them feel the need to present their best selves on their primary account—perfect pictures, celebratory moments and support for serious causes. However, they are also still teenagers. Sometimes they just want to be goofy or weird. So, they create a finsta, that is, a fake Instagram account. Here, the audience is limited to only other finstas of their closest friends, so that they can express their unedited selves to a more intimate audience.

It is easy to create a new account with a limited audience, but it is hard to keep your audience limited once you get going. Sometimes, you will meet people in real life who will ask to connect with you on social media. Often, this is an awkward moment where most people can't decline the request. Having separate accounts for Community and Connection lets you easily manage this problem. Give your Connection profile only to those whom you want to have in your inner circle. Treat your Community profile as you would the classifieds section in a newspaper. Only post that which you are comfortable knowing that the whole town could be reading tomorrow.

CHOOSE YOUR IDENTITY

As we've seen in the previous chapter, managing your identity can be a powerful way to enforce privacy preferences. Many social media platforms allow you to use pseudonyms. This means you can use them under a pretend name and not connect the account to your real identity. Pseudonymous accounts offer you identity flexibility. You can always reveal your name and make it your public account if you wish.

Pseudonymous accounts are best suited for Fraternity, where we are learning about new topics or engaging in discussions online. The obvious benefit is that they air-gap your real identity from the consequences of any conflict your pseudonymous account may stumble into. Having a pseudonymous account also helps you loosen up and really act as a beginner.

Pseudonymous accounts are also useful if you want more control over the feed you consume, especially if you want to use social media for Entertainment. For most of us, our social media feeds are maybe 10 per cent personal updates from friends, and 90 per cent a mess of news, commentary on the news, activism, celebrity gossip, memes from accounts that we joined as a joke and marketing for brands, etc. Every time you decide to scroll through this mess, there's no telling what mood you'll come out with.

As we will explain later in this chapter, researchers from DeepMind, Google's super specialized AI research firm, have shown that once the algorithm has selected a certain kind of content for you, it is very hard to break out of the mould in the eyes of the recommendation algorithm.

Use an alternate pseudonymous account that only subscribes to things that relax you, rather than overwhelm you. If this account's feed starts to degenerate, you can abandon it and open another one.

FORGET

The idea of Ephemerality is useful in social media as well. Recently, most platforms have moved to a 'stories' format of posting, where the post disappears in 24 hours or so. This increases our privacy tremendously. When we post about more intimate areas of our lives such as where we eat or where we are travelling, we reveal a lot more than we like. Especially, with a whole timeline of such posts, we cannot fully know what a malignant actor might be able to derive about us.

In September 2020, a cybersecurity expert was able to decipher the location of a secret bunker from just one picture. The picture showed some mountain peaks and a helicopter taking off. Anonymous sleuths on the internet were able to identify the make and the maximum range of the helicopter, as well as its take-off spot from publicly available data and reverse image searches. The cybersecurity expert then used Google Maps to identify the peaks which were visible and drew some perspective lines to figure out where the hidden bunker was!

Data is weird that way. Each of our individual posts may not reveal much, but taken in aggregate, it could reveal something even we don't know. Moreover, if not the data itself, the meta-data—when we post, how often we post, where we post from, etc.—also tells a story about us. The easiest protection against this unbounded risk is to create a bound on how long the data is 'live' for. Posting stories on social media allows us to keep our privacy by reducing this risk to 24 hours.

The flip side of course is that these ephemeral formats also create the craving for more social media. For those consuming content, it creates the incentive to check in regularly, because of the short half-life of the content. Similarly, for content creators, it requires them to keep posting to stay visible.

Over time, from the pages-long discussion forums of the early internet, to now with TikTok, the format in which we communicate has become a race to the bottom towards ever shorter attention spans. This isn't coincidental. Just like the slot machines from Chapter 4, one way to keep us hooked is to increase the speed of play. TikTok, Instagram/WhatsApp Stories, YouTube Shorts—all have adopted the latest 15–30 second vertical, auto-advancing, full-screen video format.

Even with every strategy we outlined here implemented rigorously, it is genuinely hard to not get hooked to the short format videos that are popular these days. This is why the path to *bitfulness* doesn't just stop at our own use of social media.

If we're going to really fix our relationship with technology, we need to fix the fundamental dynamic.

THE FUNDAMENTAL DYNAMIC

Underneath every social network, there is a fundamental problem to solve. Out of the literally millions of things posted every second online, social media companies need to select the exact content that would most engage each of their users. Social networks solve this by building recommendation engines.

The belief is that the more data a company has about an individual, the better this engine understands the taste of that individual. Like the Netflix documentary *Social Dilemma* depicted, with more data, it can create deep psychological profiles and recommend the exact content that would resonate with you or change your mind.

This is not entirely incorrect, but it is not exactly correct either.

The primary asset of any social network is its social graph. The social graph is basically a dataset representative of all user behaviour that happens on the social network. First of all, all individual accounts on the social network are nodes of the graph, as are all the posts, pictures and other objects on the social network. Every interaction between your account and a post, picture or another account is stored as an edge of the graph. Over time, a vast and complex maze of connections emerges.

Recommendation engines are typically built using machine learning over the social graph. Specifically, the most common machine learning technique to recommend content, or even people to follow, is called collaborative filtering.

Collaborative filtering is simple to understand. Each of us ends up creating a footprint on the internet based on our activity. This footprint is not used to create a deeper psychological profile. Instead, your footprint is used to find other users like you. Two users whose footprints are similar are assumed to have similar interests.

THE SOCIAL GRAPH

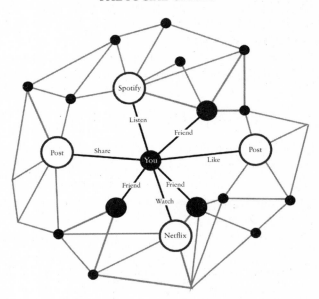

Recommendation algorithms are simply filtering people who behave like you do online. They recommend to you what people with footprints like you are seeing.

Collaborative filtering is the real secret sauce of advertising giants online, not just on the content side, but also on the monetization side. Ad platforms offer advertisers the ability to target 'similar audiences'. For example, advertisers upload a list of users who have already purchased from them. Ad platforms then use all the data they have about the users on the list to filter similar users who are not on the list. These new similar users are then served the ads that advertisers want.

Often people worry their social media is listening to their conversations. If your friend was telling you about a mattress they just bought, many are surprised they start seeing mattress ads too.

The ad companies aren't spying on either of your conversations, picking up mentions of the word 'mattress'. The mattress company your friend purchased from adds the ID of your friend to their 'similar audiences' list. Ad platforms are then simply making guesses about who is similar to your friend based on their data footprint. It is much more likely that we will buy similar goods and services, or relate with similar content as our friends. Especially those who live in the same area and have similar interests.

Collecting data is important to the model, but it is neither for mind-reading nor mind-control. It is to help with collaborative filtering. The underlying data about who you speak to is much more important from a targeting perspective, rather than what you actually said. What collaborative filtering does is to create cohorts of similar users, who are then shown similar content because of their similar history of consumption.

Your preferences and privacy are betrayed more by what people like you are doing online, rather than because they have built a deep profile of you. In fact, this creates what researchers at Google DeepMind call a 'degenerate feedback loop'. Based on a guess, the algorithm selects for you content that it thinks you will like. Even if it is not what you like, you end up going through some of the content and maybe even engaging with some of it.

Since the algorithms are now all AI, the data about our usage is fed back to the algorithm as a score of its accuracy. Because we engage with the content, no matter what we're shown, it cements the algorithm's assessment of you. Since the collaborative filtering guesses are being reinforced by its own recommendations, it may become impossible to escape the algorithm's judgement of you. The feedback loop confirms its own beliefs and becomes degenerate.

It is not a surprise, therefore, that social media is driving polarization. The fundamental dynamic at the heart of social media is dividing us into groups that each sees a different reality. If you share posts about a certain topic or follow certain people from a group, the algorithm will then encourage more of it because of degenerate feedback loops. Moreover, the algorithm then promotes content that magnifies the differences between these groups. Because that maximizes conflict and, hence, engagement.

While we do have the choice to deactivate or delete our social media, we can't control everything about it. Collaborative filtering, the attentional race to the bottom and all their consequences are not problems that we as individuals can change or fix. However, these problems affect us deeply.

The fundamental dynamic that creates the problems also makes the good parts of social media what they are. Fixing these problems will require not just one small change but probably a massive overhaul of social media. There are no easy answers, but that doesn't mean there are no answers.

We just have to ask the right question.

OUR DATA, OUR NETWORKS, OUR SELVES

Once you understand the fundamental dynamic of the social graph that really powers a social network, it leads to a bigger question.

Whether matching ads to users or showing personalized feeds, companies are mostly using collaborative filtering to recommend content. This means, it is not your data or my data in an individual sense that is valuable, it is *our* data that has the most value. The social graph reveals so much more about us as a species, than any one of our individual data sets alone ever could. The value derived from the whole is much greater than the sum of the parts. Hence, the bigger question:

Why do a handful of companies decide who benefits and in what way from *our* data?

The bargain of social media was supposed to be that we get a stage and an audience, and in return, they show us a few ads. In reality, we're giving them something much more valuable—our social graph. All the problems we see on social media—misinformation, polarization, abuse, etc.—stem at least in part from what recommendation engines have been built atop *our* social graph.

This is a question that we need to ask not just of recommendation systems, but of the technology industry as a whole. All the new Artificial Intelligence (AI) technologies fall primarily into three basic paradigms—supervised learning, unsupervised learning and reinforcement learning. Reinforcement learning learns by playing games against itself, such as AlphaGo did to defeat the world's best Go player. However, the other two paradigms depend on data. Data that *we* generate. Yet, we neither have a share nor a say in how these algorithms profit off of us, segregate us or otherwise affect us.

It becomes more perplexing when you consider that data is non-rivalrous and cheap to duplicate. George Bernard Shaw explained what non-rivalrous means most simply.

'If you have an apple and I have an apple, and we exchange these apples then you and I will still each have one apple. But if you have an idea and I have an idea, and we exchange these ideas, then each of us will have two ideas.'

You can't create economic value from something that is not scarce. To create scarcity, one has to ensure that the subset of user data they have is meaningfully unique from data that others have.

Google has a large, unique collection of user search data because it has more than 92 per cent market share of online search. In exchange for search results, we tell the search bar things we probably do not tell our closest friends. Facebook has unique social data. We tell Facebook who we are friends with and whom we follow. Our interactions further betray which of these bonds are stronger and which are not.

We cannot limit the creation of data. Our every online action and interaction will leave a trail. In fact, sometimes we would want this data to exist for our own sake. Imagine if your bank lost data about your transaction history. What we need is more control over what happens after that generation. Should it be stored? Who gets to store it? What can they use it for? What if we don't like what they do with it? Can we ask them to delete it?

Companies like Facebook and TikTok have control over the social infrastructure. This enables them to get our data and prevent the competition from having that unique subset of user data. Also, why wouldn't they? It makes definite business sense to do so. Anyone else in their position would've done the same.

The original sin of the internet was that we decided to sell our attention to pay for the missing infrastructure of the internet. Today, this logic has given rise to a few players who essentially own the critical infrastructure of the internet. The owners of this infrastructure are using *our* data to further *their* control. No matter what we do individually, we can't fix this till we fix the vacuum at the heart of the internet. This is why The Third Crisis is a collective problem, and we need to find solutions collectively.

Social media is likely to remain a broken place till we make sure that *our* data is on *our* networks, so that we can be truly free to be *our selves*.

PART THREE

THE COLLECTIVE

13

SLIPPERY SLOPES OF SCALE

EXPONENTIALS

In mid-April of 2020, when most countries struggled to get the testing infrastructure in place for the COVID-19 pandemic, an intriguing news item found its way around the Indian internet. A technology developed by three young bioinformatics students from Mumbai was being piloted by a university in Rome. The technology could, allegedly, diagnose COVID-19 from voice recordings of the patients. Put simply, you would speak into a smartphone, and it would tell you whether you were infected with the coronavirus or not.

If you're reading this in the year 2021 or beyond, you'd be looking at the news of a voice-based AI test sceptically. If there was a voice-based AI test for coronavirus, we'd have seen it by now. But that wisdom is the gift of hindsight. In mid-April 2020, India was still in week 3 of a very stringent lockdown. All news channels were busy explaining the nature of exponential growth curves to audiences. What seemed like a few cases today would become many thousands of cases in two weeks. In a couple of months, we'd be looking at hundreds of thousands of cases. Rapid testing was crucial to flattening the boundless, ever upward-climbing growth curve of COVID-19.

The authors of this book are unqualified to predict the efficacy or accuracy of this voice-based diagnosis technology, and it also is beside the point. We're using this story as a springboard to ask a different question: what would happen next if this technology had actually delivered even *some* of what it promised?

If we suspend our disbelief and imagine that such a technology was possible, it would be a breakthrough discovery in April 2020. At that time, a cheap, widely available, non-invasive, self-administered test could've genuinely changed the course of the global pandemic. Even if the test wasn't 98 per cent accurate, and needed reconfirmation via an RT-PCR, it would still give us more and better information to make wiser policy choices. It could be deployed globally because of the nature of digital technologies. Even if the voice-based test was not accurate, but simply *good enough*, it would still be a powerful tool in civilization's arsenal against COVID-19. Individuals would be able to check on their own health and reduce their anxiety.

Instead of blunt lockdowns at a national scale that crippled many economies, countries could selectively target and enforce lockdowns in hotspots. Even in countries with a milder lockdown, businesses were still crippled by the public's lack of trust in the safety of going outside. Physical businesses would be able to screen patrons at the door by checking their voices. Along with masks and social distancing, this test would help ensure confidence of the public in their establishment.

This voice-based diagnostic technology could collectively save billions of dollars and maybe tens of thousands of lives. The advantages of this hypothetical scenario are obvious and easy to imagine. What we don't usually imagine are the side effects. What would be the path of this technology from an early pilot to potentially testing everyone worldwide? What would be the other consequences of taking that path?

We said in Chapter 3 that the real crisis is that *how* we are going digital will lead to an imbalance of power. We want to explain what we mean through a hypothetical scenario. For this next part, imagine that it is April 2020 and that you are in the driver's seat of this ground-breaking innovation. If you had just invented this technology to diagnose COVID-19, you'd be asking the obvious question—how do you get this technology to everyone, everywhere fast?

In Silicon Valley parlance, you'd be asking—How do I scale?

STAYING SAFE

In startup culture, 'bigness' is proof of goodness.

This is often the first and the foremost defence against criticism of internet companies. Supporters claim companies wouldn't be big if they weren't innovative and customer-centric. They claim that to become big, a company must be good at what they do and serve a real customer need.

The argument isn't entirely without merit. No tech company can grow to a meaningful size if it doesn't actually solve a consumer need for a reasonable number of people. But once they have found a consumer need, to grow to a stratospheric size requires a different approach.

To demonstrate, let's go back to the example of the Artificial Intelligence-enabled, voice-based COVID-19 diagnostic test and see how you would scale this product.

First things first, you pick a name for your new invention. 'Artificial Intelligence enabled voice-based COVID-19 diagnostic test' is quite a mouthful, so you choose 'SaySafe'. It is easy to remember, a clever play on 'stay safe' and highlights the voice-based nature of your technology. Most importantly, the web domain saysafe.ai is available.

You built the pilot using your university's computers. For the real world, you're going to need to put your algorithms on dedicated hardware to ensure they run reliably. You have a few critical choices to make on distribution. You could install the technology on specialized, portable devices so that people can carry out this test anywhere, anytime, even without the internet. Imagine Amazon's Echo smart speakers, but for the singular purpose of COVID-19 detection.

However, it is April 2020 and the manufacturing hub for such devices, China, is under a severe lockdown. Global supply chains have been disrupted. Suppose you try to make a dedicated device. In that case, you'd be unlikely to make and ship enough devices in the pandemic for your technology to benefit enough people. Besides, as any tech pundit will often tell you, hardware doesn't scale as well as software.

You realize that people already have microphones in their smartphones. It would be best if you simply made your test work on the internet and let people use their own devices to access your technology via an app. This distribution method has advantages of maximum reach and minimum maintenance. You only have to make it once and can then deploy it everywhere. Serving the app online allows you to collect data and improve your model over time. The updates make their way to all users immediately—no waiting to buy another version or need to replace their devices. The problem is you've never made anything that can handle the volumes you're targeting. You start looking for good engineers to help you.

To get engineers on this task, you're going to have to pay them. You don't have the money to spare for that, nor does your university. A research grant would take weeks, if not months, to come through. Given that this technology can save billions of dollars, your professor suggests that you build a start-up and raise venture capital. The government had recently launched a mobile app to help entrepreneurs such as yourself set up a new company in under a day. On Monday, you register your company online and email VC firms. Because your app is so timely, they all want to see you on Zoom on Wednesday.

The VCs go over a demo and are impressed. They all tell you that they've seen four other companies trying to do what you do, but you are ahead on the pilot due to your university's data. If they give you the money, they want to make sure you get a lead in the market and retain it. They ask, 'what is your business model?' You say you're going to charge per test to cover the costs of servers and engineers. They tell you that this is a bad idea. One of the other four companies might charge lower than you and people will opt for the cheaper test. 'What's important,' one of the VCs says, 'is that you show consistent growth. How about making the test free? HealthTech is a hot space right now, you can always figure out how to make money later'.

You decide that it is much more important to let people know their COVID-19 diagnosis than make money. Moreover, the VCs seem reluctant to give you money if you charge people and eager to sign a cheque if you don't. You see this as a win–win and accept an offer from a reputed VC firm. In return, you hand over some equity, a board seat and agree to hire a 'growth hacker'. You're excited to have the money to hire the engineers you wanted and get to work.

It is now June, and the SaySafe online app is ready to go. Customers log in with their email address or phone number. You give them a fixed prompt to read. They simply read out the text in their own voice, record it and send it to your cloud. An AI algorithm analyses the fresh voice sample against previous voice samples from that user on the cloud. Some of your most eager users submit their temperature every day or submit their results if an RT-PCR test came back positive. The algorithm is continuously tweaked by your engineers based on this feedback. People begin to use your service, and in just a few days you've done more than 10,000 tests.

Your user base is growing fast. With the volumes you're expecting, you're not going to be able to serve all your users without footing a costly server bill. Your algorithms need quite a lot of computational power, and your engineers need to be paid astronomical salaries. You begin to see your bank balance dwindle. So you go to a bigger VC firm which offers you more money. Once again, they ask for equity, and another board seat and that you hire a 'Head of Business' in exchange for the money you need to keep going. You had started this company with the vision of ubiquitous testing, and you're still far from that goal. So you agree, sign the deal, and soon the money hits your bank account. You get back to work.

When you reach a million users, your new Head of Business asks what SaySafe does with the user once the test is over. You explain that you're a diagnostics app and after you show the results your job is done. The new business head looks disappointed with you. He explains that this is a wasted opportunity. 'We're not a diagnostics company, we're a Health Tech company. We need to leverage technology to provide our users with the best end-to-end healthcare solutions.'

Your business head recommends that SaySafe start diagnosing for more than merely COVID-19. Lots of other diseases can be detected by voice. If the results are positive, SaySafe can directly connect users to the hospitals and clinics around them. By asking users to give data about their insurance, SaySafe can even recommend hospitals covered by your provider. SaySafe can earn money by getting independent doctors and hospitals to bid for incoming leads from your diagnostics app. This will all be free for users, since you get paid by the doctors.

Your board of directors, largely comprising the two VCs who funded you, thinks this is a wonderful idea. The VCs recommend you raise more money to grow the team and hire the new engineers you now need. You also realize you now need a 'Head of Product' to manage all the engineers you hired.

Patients who login to check their COVID-19 status and are now also being diagnosed for other diseases at no additional cost. Doctors and hospitals who had seen fewer patients due to the lockdown start lowering prices, outbidding each other to get your leads. Since you allow users to conveniently book appointments, you see some growth in the number of users. It helps that booking through your platform is cheaper than booking with the clinic directly, thanks to the money provided by your VCs.

Your head of product made it a point to measure every little detail of how users are behaving by recording their data. People are logging in less frequently to check if they are sick, he points out. They are also getting stressed by worrying about COVID every day, so they're avoiding the voice tests. Good for them, but bad for SaySafe's business. You still are spending on salaries and servers but don't have enough income. Your board suggests you need to keep the growth going if you don't want to run out of money.

Someone in your engineering team suggests that SaySafe can pivot into mental health diagnostics. 'What if we could replace the fixed prompts with open-ended questions instead? Prompts like "How are you feeling today?" or "What's on your mind?" While we will continue to use the voice samples to diagnose their diseases, we will use AI to recognize variations in stress levels day-to-day. I've already written a proposal and can help you present it to the board.' The engineers are excited. Your board is elated. An investor is willing to sign another big cheque if you expand from merely Health Tech into the growing 'Wellness' industry.

Still, SaySafe won't sustain its lofty valuation if you can't convert some of that traffic into revenue. You call your team for brainstorming, and many suggest selling the data. You put your foot down and say that constitutes a breach of trust. You don't want to sell user data; you're not *that* kind of company. So you agree to sell ads instead. However, the ads are targeted to users depending on what they said, to make them more relevant. Your team starts building the upgrades.

The clickthrough rates on these ads initially were high, but in a few months, they begin to fall as people grow tired of the ads. The board pulls you up for not delivering on the promised numbers. You are now desperate for anything that will turn around the revenue numbers. When getting more users was no longer an option, someone from the ads team had another suggestion on increasing revenues. 'People aren't just using SaySafe for health anymore. They're discussing their problems like they would with a friend. We know who's thinking of buying a car, who's thinking of taking a vacation, etc. Moreover, the daily prompts guide what they talk about. What if we could allow advertisers to pay for prompts to their target audience. An e-commerce retailer would pay to ask someone in their mid-twenties "What are you thinking of buying for your mother this Mother's Day?" etc. This could be as big for us as video ads were for Facebook.'

Your board approves the idea, and your team implements the feature. Slowly, your prompts start driving sales more than ads. Soon, your valuation triples. The public starts worshipping you as a tech genius.

What started as a diagnostic app becomes a full-fledged surveillance tool. Eventually, even surveillance does not suffice for the manic growth that everyone expected of you. The only way to surpass that expectation was to incept thoughts into the minds of your users. You started in April 2020 with a wonderful idea and a genuine desire to change the world. In a few short years, you realize that your nightmare is that you *did* change the world but not in the way you intended.

The specifics of this hypothetical example are deliberately far-fetched, but the trajectory is not that far from reality. 'How do we scale?' is a fundamental question every new technology or business idea faces at some point in time. Thirty years ago, when the worldwide web didn't exist, there was a different playbook for information technology products to grow. But over the last thirty years, we've seen various models emerge, fail and reinvent themselves till a particular model has become the *de facto* method to succeed.

The model is to scale at any cost or perish trying. Profits are not what they're chasing; an unshakeable control over a large part of the market is what they are after. VCs invest billions of dollars in these start-ups, who in turn subsidize users by providing services for free, or cheaper than analogue competitors to grow their online business. Often, this means the companies are making losses happily. Once they reach a certain size, economies of scale and network effects work together to cement their market position. This strategy has become the default across many domains and products—whether online advertising (Google/Facebook), digital payments (Alipay/Wechat), ridesharing (Uber/Ola) or food delivery (Zomato/Swiggy).

This strategy has many names, but let's stick with the name that Reid Hoffman gave it, *blitzscaling*.

BLITZSCALING

Reid Hoffman was one of the co-founders of PayPal. PayPal was one of the early successes of the internet. Veterans from PayPal, such as Elon Musk or Peter Thiel, would go on to become successful tech entrepreneurs with multiple ventures. Hoffman went on to found LinkedIn, which was eventually sold to Microsoft for US$34 billion. Hoffman coined the term *blitzscaling* for this strategy of dazzling growth fuelled by burning investor money.

According to Hoffman, 'Blitzscaling means that you're willing to sacrifice efficiency for speed, without waiting to achieve certainty on whether the sacrifice will pay off. If classic start-up growth is about slowing your rate of descent as you try to assemble your plane, blitzscaling is about assembling that plane faster, then strapping on and igniting a set of jet engines (and possibly their afterburners) while you're still building the wings.'

If the proximity to 'blitzkrieg' bristles, do remember that he coined this term in early 2016. This was a different era. This was before news of the Cambridge Analytica scandal broke and the public mood soured on tech. At that time, these startups were darlings, not just on Wall Street, but in public opinion too. Reid Hoffman wasn't writing a takedown of tech by comparing it to a Nazi Germany strategy. He was praising the strategy for its counter-intuitive nature.

As Hoffman put it in an April 2016 interview to *Harvard Business Review*, 'I have obvious hesitations about the World War II association with the term "blitzkrieg". However, the intellectual parallels are so close that it is very informative. Before blitzkrieg emerged as a military tactic, armies didn't advance beyond their supply lines, which limited their speed. The theory of the blitzkrieg was that if you carried only what you absolutely needed, you could move very, very fast, surprise your enemies, and win. Once you got halfway to your destination, you had to decide whether to turn back or to abandon the lines and go on. Once you made the decision to move forward, you were all in. You won big or lost big. Blitzscaling adopts a similar perspective.'

What's wrong with scaling? Inherently, nothing. Economics has always lauded efficiencies of scale as a way of increasing productivity and prosperity. Lots of companies borrow money from the stock markets or through bond markets to grow bigger and compete. In fact, to make the distinction clear, Hoffman calls this regular kind of growth *fastscaling*. Fastscaling is where companies sacrifice some efficiency to favour growth. The catch here is that when a company which has figured out its market and product, but is now trying to grow market share scales, it is only considered fast. It is not *blitz*.

To be *blitz*, you have to deliberately throw caution to the wind and take huge bets on things you don't fully understand. According to Hoffman, 'When a market is up for grabs, the risk isn't inefficiency—the risk is playing it too safe'. Hoffman recommends *blitzscaling* precisely for those new technologies whose consequences and impact on society are not fully understood. If you're hesitant, then blitzscaling start-ups is not for you. 'Do or Die', reminds Hoffman.

Where you stand on a matter depends ultimately on where you sit. Investing in blitzscaling companies gives huge returns in a *blitz*. As a general of the tech industry and a partner at the VC firm Greylock Ventures, Hoffman is glorifying a strategy that typifies what he likes to invest in. However, if you were one of the incumbents being disrupted, maybe the other World War II metaphor that you would find more apt for this strategy would be *kamikaze*.

Hoffman is by no means an outlier, or the lone purveyor of this strategy. Even before Hoffman, others have said essentially the same thing. One of the biggest names to promote the same strategy has been Peter Thiel, another co-founder of PayPal. In his very popular book, *Zero to One*, Peter Thiel essentially advocates a similar approach in an effort to 'escape' competition, 'Monopoly is the condition of every successful business . . . All happy companies are different: each one earns a monopoly by solving a unique problem. All failed companies are the same: they failed to escape competition.' Hoffman spoke of the process, whereas Thiel is explicit about the end goal—a unique monopoly.

Blitzscaling might be a great strategy to differentiate yourself from your fast-scaling peers. However, if you blitzscale, it usually means that your competition has to blitzscale too or they will get left behind in winner-take-all races. As a society, we all hurtle towards an uncertain and risky future at jet speed with the afterburners on. One of the blitzscaling entrepreneurs might even succeed in building the wings, but no one really has a working steering and absolutely no one is building the brakes.

We believe the real problem here is the one left unsaid. When chasing a unique monopoly, or trying to grow really fast, you enter a dangerous game we call the Slippery Slopes of Scale. By making certain decisions early on, such as raising capital that's premised on hyper-growth, entrepreneurs essentially force their own hand. This is what we wanted to demonstrate with the SaySafe example. It is not evil people looking to conquer the world, but reasonable people trying to do something good that causes The Third Crisis. Burning bridges, going big or going home, whatever metaphor you may choose to phrase it, the strategy is designed to be self-fulfilling. You may have your initial doubts, but once you commit to it, you really have no way out except to go further in.

The problem goes back to the internet's original sin. Because there was no real way to send money on the internet, businesses had to take their money from elsewhere. This money from investors came with the expectation of phenomenal growth, and even today, technology start-ups are synonymous with a chance at rapid, astronomical wealth creation. Advertising made the first wave of internet businesses such as Google and Facebook free.

However, since mobile devices and the internet have become more commonplace, a second, and more pervasive internet business model has emerged called 'Aggregation'. If we don't address it soon, this model threatens to spread The Third Crisis from a few industries, such as online advertising, to every industry and job.

AGGREGATION

Conducting commerce on the internet makes a lot of sense.

For consumers, e-commerce provides the widest variety of suppliers. For sellers, it reaches the widest audiences. However, as economists would say, the marginal utility of every additional choice quickly falls. Add enough choice and it may even turn negative.

Humans are not good at dealing with infinite choice. Once you could buy anything from anyone, anywhere, it became harder to decide what to buy, from where. Thus, the internet gave rise to a second kind of business model to solve a problem it had itself created. This business model was aggregation. It involved aggregating sellers and matching them with interested buyers.

The adoption of the smartphone has spurred the aggregation model to expand from simply selling products to selling services. Once we all had a portable computer in our pockets, we could use it to order cabs, get food delivered, and purchase other services on the fly.

The fundamental aim of the aggregation model is to create an online marketplace where buyers and sellers transact. The transaction infrastructure is provided by the aggregator and is called the platform.

Aggregators solve two key problems for e-commerce transactions—Discovery and Trust. Discovery is the ability to find the right thing that you need from the right sellers. Trust is making sure that both parties are playing fair and don't commit fraud. Many tech companies deploy the aggregation model. AirBnB, Alibaba, Amazon, eBay, Etsy, GrubHub, Oyo, Ola, Swiggy, Uber, UberEats, Zomato, etc., are all aggregators. The difference in their approaches is how they solve for transactions, discovery and trust.

Online shopping for products is often cheaper. E-commerce shortens the supply chain and brings in efficiencies of scale. Inventory & logistics can be optimized, wastage & returns can be reduced, and automation can drive down costs.

However, the fundamental cost of driving a taxi does not reduce when one company aggregates millions of them. So what makes the aggregation model so popular for services?

Because it is the model most amenable to blitzscaling. The aggregation model relies on two ideas. The first is that aggregation will cause the markets to concentrate. Second, you can speed up that concentration by blitzscaling.

Aggregation naturally encourages concentration in any industry due to Network Effects. If there were two platforms, all else being equal, as a buyer, you'd prefer the one with more sellers. Similarly, as a seller, you'd prefer a platform with more buyers. Basically, when we want to participate in a network, the bigger it already is, the more attractive it is. Any platform that is able to take a lead on either buyers or sellers, therefore, usually manages to draw the other side. The big networks get bigger, and the winners take all. This results in a virtuous cycle of growth, helping these companies grow even faster.

NETWORK EFFECTS

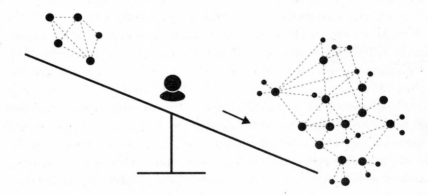

Each user finds the bigger network more attractive.
By design, the winner takes all.

Network effects are everywhere in internet companies because they offer a defence against competition. Most famously, Amazon explicitly made network effects their strategy. They called this model the 'flywheel'. Better customer experience—wide selection, two-day shipping, easy returns, etc.—means more traffic, which improves the variety of products by attracting sellers and makes overheads cheaper. The money saved is invested in making the customer experience even better, driving even more traffic.

The Blitzscaling strategy combines very well with network effects. VCs bankroll companies to build a pool of sellers and buyers inorganically, without worrying about near-term profits. While capital remains cheap, these tech companies are often subsidizing the real costs of goods and services. The Indian start-up ecosystem is awash with stories of how people have gotten goods and services at below costs, because of cashbacks and promotional offers by blitzscaling start-ups.

Our personal favourite (possibly apocryphal) example is the gentleman who wanted to move his bed from one apartment to another in Delhi. Simply hiring a truck and labour would have cost him nearly a thousand rupees. Instead, he had the genius idea of selling it on OLX and using another account to purchase it from himself. OLX took zero fees and paid for the transportation and labour. He used PayTM to pay for the purchase, which gave him a cashback for the purchase. He moved his bed, and ended up netting 200 rupees profit, funded by blitzscaling VCs.

Analogue competitors find it hard to compete with Blitzscaling. Without access to the kind of deep and cheap capital that internet startups get, these analogue competitors tend to fall behind. This increases our dependence on these big platforms and accelerates The Third Crisis. Only those who are playing a well-capitalized blitzscaling strategy can compete, but network effects make even this competition hard to sustain. The result in the long run, one way or another, is concentration.

Once demand concentrates on their infrastructure, these aggregators have a much larger role to play than simply connecting a buyer and a seller. They have a thumb on the scales. They can redirect traffic to their preferred sellers, extract fees or even compete with independent sellers. They own critical data such as user purchases across all sellers, which is not available to any individual seller on the marketplace. Moreover, even when consumers don't purchase, *only* the aggregator knows what people are searching for and clicking on. Aggregators, hence, know consumer interest and trends better than any seller.

Information about what sells is incredibly valuable. Independent sellers invest what little capital they have in experiments with new products and positioning to learn about consumer demand. Aggregators get this knowledge off of the sellers' backs for free. This can be problematic since some aggregators have in-house brands that compete with their own sellers for user demand.

If you think you're simply a consumer and are not going to be affected by aggregation, think again.

The move to e-commerce has been accelerated. The supply chain of products was already being rewired. The massive opportunity now is in the supply chain of labour.

Your income is either the result of selling goods directly in a market or indirectly as an employee, selling your labour as a service. Somewhere upstream or downstream of you in the supply chain is a tech company planning to aggregate the market. Unless you earn your income purely from capital such as being a landlord, or an investor, aggregation will eventually affect you. It has already happened to cab drivers and delivery riders. There is no reason why aggregation can't happen to accountants, brokers, consultants, doctors and engineers too.

For that much power over the fate of so many businesses and employees, there is hardly any oversight or rules that require aggregators to compete fairly.

EVITABLE

When asked about the disruption Amazon caused to the books and publishing industry, CEO Jeff Bezos has an oft-repeated quote, 'Amazon did not happen to the book business. The future happened to the book business.'

Many, like Bezos, do not believe that The Third Crisis is a man-made problem. They claim that the changes to individual lives and entire industries are due to more powerful, mysterious forces outside of themselves. Jeff Bezos blames 'the future' for the plight of publishers today. He claims that Amazon is merely the messenger of an *inevitable* disruption.

According to this world view shared by some in the industry, the future is what it is. Its consequences on people's lives and livelihoods are unfortunate in the same manner that being in a tornado's path is. Stand in their way, and they will imply you simply do not understand the future nor their role in it. Internet companies claim that the rewiring of every business, not just books, is inevitable. They are merely trying to deliver the future the way they do everything else— guaranteed one-day delivery and free shipping.

To their credit, they aren't *entirely* wrong. Most people would agree that calling a taxi by wandering on the streets and waving your hand is a lot more unpleasant and uncertain than ordering a taxi from an app.

The catch is that this does not make an Uber or an Amazon *inevitable*. In the long run, most things will get digitized. But the way they get digitized is not an immutable law of physics. The current set of aggregators are simply *a* model amongst many others. Usually, they end up becoming *the* model because they are the blitzscaling-friendly model.

Founders, VCs, tech employees and other beneficiaries of the Slippery Slopes of Scale want you to believe that 'the future' is an inevitable force of progress. They want you to believe what they're doing is innovative. Therefore, the business practices that go along with the innovation must be justified. Businesses today use questionable practices to get more users and then use the growing number of users to justify their practices.

If you want to find an honest admission from the internet startups of what they are really up to, you'll find it in surprising places. Uber's former CEO and founder, Travis Kalanick, speaking at a conference in 2014, before the public mood turned on Uber, said 'We're in a political campaign, and the candidate is Uber and the opponent is an asshole named Taxi.' Opponents would disagree on who the asshole is but would agree that the structure of our economy is a public affair.

This is about politics and power, as much as it is about innovation and technology.

In the early years of information technologies, decisions and compromises were made in designing the internet. There was a vacuum in the centre of the internet, which we overcame with the original sin of choosing advertising. It is now being compounded by aggregation. We are where we are then, not because of the future, but because of the past.

Even though it does feel like we're headed towards a winner-take-all future, powered by a jet engine with afterburners on, there's still reason to hope. The point of this chapter is to convince you that the future isn't inevitable; it is an extrapolation of design choices we made in the past. As a society, we've faced similar big questions of how to design society, and often, we've come out ahead with ideas such as liberal democracy, human rights and peace winning in the long run. There's no particular reason to believe we can't do the same again.

Therefore, it is not *the* future that happened to the books business, but merely *a* future, favourable to some tech companies. The next two chapters describe two alternative models for a future that do not slide us up the Slippery Slopes of Scale. We want to describe the alternatives for our future, because we cannot predict it. The choice of what future we get is still open and depends on how we act as a collective.

To know *the* future, it is wise to look at the past. History has repeatedly shown us that this particular future where a handful of people hold all the power is, in fact, very *evitable*.

14

CRYPTOMANIA

DESIGNED-IN DANGERS

The enduring narrative around technology, especially touted by those who build it, is that it is a tool, neither good nor bad in itself. They claim that the toxic patterns in our relationship with technology are problems arising from how people use these tools.

Before 1965, this was precisely the argument around fatal automobile accidents. The American automobile industry was very similar to the tech industry of today. It had consolidated into 3 companies. Over 93 per cent of the cars sold in America and 48 per cent of those sold worldwide were American, majorly sold by these three companies. The number of fatal accidents had been rising every year. Many in the industry argued that *it is not the cars, it is the drivers*. The industry narrative was that the drivers should be driving under the speed limits or paying more attention while on the road.

In 1965, consumer advocate Ralph Nader wrote a book called *Unsafe at Any Speed: The Designed-In Dangers of the American Automobile*. The title itself gives away the key argument—It wasn't the drivers, it was the *design* of the car itself. Chasing ever cheaper and more fuel-efficient cars, the automobile manufacturers were prioritizing costs over safety. The specific examples in the book are still challenged by some experts. However, few doubt the results of the conversations that followed. In a 2015 article in *The New York*

Times, a reporter summarized the changes fifty years after the book was published.

> A host of new safety requirements led—often after stiff opposition—to new technologies such as airbags, anti-lock brakes, electronic stability control and, recently, rear-view cameras and automatic braking.
>
> Indeed, the death rate has dropped strikingly. In 1965, there were about five deaths for every 100 million miles travelled according to the traffic safety agency. In 2014, the most recent year available, there was one death for every 100 million miles.

We believe it is time for a similar conversation in technology. Yes, when someone posts graphic or violent messages on social media, it is not Facebook or Mark Zuckerberg who got them to do so. However, the fact that millions of people feel addicted to their phones or social media is not because we are using the tools wrong. In fact, this is the outcome of these tools doing *exactly* what they were designed to do.

There is no denying that these platforms *are* tools. However, that doesn't absolve internet startups of responsibility from the consequences of the platform's usage. Every little design detail they choose has a ripple effect on our lives as consumers and businesses. How they configure our software determines how we spend our time, money and attention online. Just a few tweaks can make lasting changes in the moods and lives of billions of people, affecting our lives and livelihoods in profound ways. In short, the design of these tools is the design of our individual and collective future. As long as we can change the design of these tools, no *one* future is inevitable.

The question then becomes—how can we design our technology to serve all of us rather than serve its makers?

KNIFE TO A GUNFIGHT

Regulations are an oft mentioned solution to make technology serve us all.

It is a widely accepted position that these companies need to be regulated. In fact, the biggest of 'Big Tech' actually *welcome* regulation. The debate comes down to the finer points of *how* these companies should be regulated.

Aggregators find lacunae in existing regulations. Uber, Lyft or Ola may fight amongst each other for a market share of ride-sharing, but they are all competing against existing taxicab operators, public transport and car ownership. By using elaborate but legal arrangements, aggregators manage to shirk responsibilities traditional employers and service providers have to bear. Moreover, they claim this is progress and, thus, *inevitable*.

When the pandemic hit, Uber and Lyft contractors in the US weren't eligible for unemployment insurance, because Uber and Lyft hadn't paid those taxes claiming drivers were contractors. Studies have now shown that rather than decrease car ownership, ride-sharing apps increase congestion in cities. Similarly, AirBnBs and other short-term rentals can drive up rents in zoned areas. They make local housing unaffordable in tourist destinations, while simultaneously taking away tax revenues from local governments.

On their mission to blitzscale, some even go a step further into potential malpractice. The US-based food delivery aggregator GrubHub set up as many as 23,000 misleading websites for restaurants on its platform without the consent of the restaurant owners. They optimized these websites to be the top hits on search engines, sabotaging the restaurant's own web presence. However, this fake website had GrubHub's phone number instead of the restaurant's. Customers believe they are placing an order directly at their local restaurants. Whereas, they were actually placing it on an automated line set up by the aggregators. The restaurants still got charged commissions on these orders.

Governments try to bring into effect newer legislations to level the playing field but can be often outgunned by the aggregators. Aggregators are able to finance both legal challenges as well as policy advocacy efforts. In California, Uber, Lyft and Doordash came together and spent US$205 million to campaign for a ballot initiative called Prop-22, wielding more than 10x the funding of the campaign against Prop-22.

Prop-22 allowed these particular aggregators to seek exemption from a law that required them to classify their delivery and transportation agents as employees. Instead, they created a new category of employment called the contract gig worker. Contract gig workers are not afforded the same protections as full-time employees.

Of course, many gig workers and platform sellers are happy with the way things are right now. When the tide is rising, it lifts all boats. The problems start on the downturn when the low prices and high commissions do not leave enough on the table. During the pandemic lockdowns, food delivery apps became the primary source of orders for struggling restaurants. Without walk-in customers, the price of commissions on the delivery orders pinched already struggling restaurants.

Tech companies like regulations once they are big, because they impose disproportionately larger costs on those smaller than them. Moderation of content, for example, takes human reviewers or massive investment in AI systems. Both of these investments see efficiencies of scale. AI systems, further, get better with more data. Regulations that are not designed to be progressive and proportional have the counter-intended effect of reducing competition from smaller platforms. Thereby, increasing concentration and aggravating The Third Crisis.

Instead of a reactive approach to the excesses of the technology industry, we can orient policy towards proactive measures. Internet startups adapt and respond to changes in the regulatory landscape by updating their software and their business model. Regulators are slow by design, whereas startups move with *blitz*. While the legal challenge is being disputed, analogue markets continue being eroded, and the aggregators continue to accrue network effects. Purely legal instruments will always be a step or two behind tech companies. If we want our information infrastructure to serve our goals, we need a bigger say in its design.

A few internet startups are building the core information infrastructure and networks of our digital future. Hence, they have control over critical questions about our collective well-being, such as:

How is the value generated on these platforms distributed? Who decides the pricing and the rules? What agency do users have in voicing their complaints, or exiting the platform? Who has the ultimate say in matters under dispute? Are we fine with a group of privately controlled entities taking these decisions for us?

If we want to take back control, we can't bring a knife to a gunfight. We need to bring technology to bear on this problem created by technology. Instead of trying to check power with just regulation, the answer is to build the digital infrastructure we desire, in the manner we desire. We can re-architect the infrastructure so that we can transact digitally, without centralizing market power to a handful of entities. Instead of weakly enforced laws, we can then embed the rules we desire in the code of these platforms itself.

Starting in 2009, two different ideas took root in two different parts of the world. They both put individual sovereignty at the heart of their mission to build technology for society. In the rest of this chapter, we deal with the first of those ideas—Cryptocurrencies and the decentralized web.

THE WEB 3.0

In 2009, some person (or possibly a group of people; we still don't know) by the pseudonym Satoshi Nakamoto published a white paper called 'Bitcoin: Peer-to-Peer Electronic Cash System'. This paper outlined a way in which you could send a payment from one person to another without going through a financial intermediary. Thus far, banks kept track of who had how much money in which account. The banks kept accurate records of all transactions, and in turn, they were kept honest by the central bank, the regulators and the courts.

Nakamoto described a system of maintaining this ledger in public in a way that replaced all the oversight by force of law with a trust in math. Anyone could propose an update to the ledger, but to prevent fraud, only the records that were legitimate would be accepted as valid. The legitimacy of a record was assured by the use of cryptography. Hence, Bitcoin and its successors came to be called cryptocurrencies.

The underlying principle is that instead of trusting a single authority, cryptocurrencies use some form of a consensus algorithm amongst a group of decentralized peers. That is, instead of one ledger maintained by a big bank, everyone has a copy of the ledger that they each participate in maintaining. Now, some bad actors may want to change the ledger to benefit themselves. This is where the consensus algorithms come in.

The various consensus algorithms—such as Proof of Stake or Proof of Work—all have one job. They incentivize honest behaviour in maintaining a ledger and penalize dishonest behaviour. The way each algorithm does this is slightly different and not important in this context. What we need to take away is that the primary motivation for good behaviour is financial incentives/disincentives that lead to an honest consensus amongst many distributed participants. Instead of one institution or person held accountable by the law, many people are kept honest by their own financial interests.

In the last decade, cryptocurrencies have grown to have over US$3 Trillion in market capitalization. The underlying public ledgers are now called blockchains, and are being applied to problems other than electronic peer-to-peer cash transfer. The idea is to try to rebuild the internet as a true peer-to-peer system, without centralized platforms. Technology such as blockchains is now being used to create a whole new internet, where not just financial, but many other intermediaries are eliminated. This is often referred to as the web3, and the new applications built on top of them are called decentralized apps, or dApps.

In the last few years, there has been an explosive increase in the use of cryptocurrencies. There is tremendous excitement and interest in the space, and often this leads to rising prices of tokens. Which in turn generates more returns for token holders and attracts even more people to cryptocurrency. You may have already heard some things about cryptocurrency, and you may have plenty of questions. Is it real? Is it useful? Isn't it used for terrible things, like drug trafficking, and by hackers? Will it bring world peace[1]?

We are not going to answer those questions. We feel compelled to point out that these were questions being asked about the internet in

---

[1]   In an interview at a bitcoin conference in 2021, Twitter CEO Jack Dorsey said that he believes bitcoin will bring world peace. His argument is detailed at bitfulness.com/worldpeace.

the 1990s as well. What we can say is this: there are individual ideas in cryptocurrency that make a lot of sense. Being able to maintain immutable ledgers in public, having no single point of failure, etc., are great ideas, implemented well by cryptocurrencies and will find much use in real life.

However, the playbook for legitimacy of cryptocurrencies has been the same as it was for the internet in the early 1990s. Believers of crypto, who are usually also invested in cryptocurrencies, will tell you that it is 'the future' and that the replacement of regular currency is 'inevitable'. True to form, their consensus around this belief is aligned with their own financial interests.

The real question to ask is if the underlying goods deliver what is promised on the package.

THE CRYPTOGRAPHIC PROOF OF THE PUDDING

In theory, the decentralized web has the potential to revolutionize the way we do everything. In practice, though, things are far from perfect. Scratch under the surface and you will realize that:

1. things aren't necessarily as decentralized as promised, and
2. that decentralization solves some problems, but often creates many of its own.

Although a full and detailed discussion of these topics would need a book of its own, we want to summarize the key arguments in a manner that readers unfamiliar with cryptocurrencies can follow. Thus, we will be generalizing in some places, and we encourage our readers to do their own research to dive deeper. We recommend the essay 'On Collusion' by Vitalik Butalin, the founder of the world's second-largest cryptocurrency, Ethereum. Also, none of what follows is investment advice.

First of all, Web 3.0 is a decentralized technology where, in theory, anyone can participate in the consensus building. In practice, it often becomes a plutocracy. Often, validating or verifying the public ledger is done by specialized entities that we will call 'miners' for ease of discussion. All these miners spend computational energy, or stake capital, towards building consensus on the blockchain, and some are rewarded for the work they do. Moreover, the way the incentives work, bigger miners often have a better chance of winning that reward. Becoming a miner is not yet so easy that any one of us can do it. It may require specialized equipment, and definitely requires specialized skills. This often leads to outcomes where a majority of the miners are just a small group of people who have power over what is recorded (or not) on the blockchain. Other individuals such as founders of cryptocurrencies, by virtue of their holdings and influence in the community, have a large say in what happens on the blockchain too.

This brings us to the second, even more worrying problem of collusion. The decentralized web depends on the decentralized actors not being able to coordinate easily. If enough of them could coordinate, they could rewrite the blockchain to benefit themselves at the cost of others. As long as malicious collusion is hard, it makes the 'right' outcome the easiest one to coordinate. However, in practice, since there may be only a handful of actors, collusion may not be that hard.

Anonymity—one of the key weaknesses due to which collusion is hard to defeat on the decentralized internet—is a feature that the Web 3.0 often touts as a strength. Anyone can create an account on the blockchain, without revealing who they are. This also means that *anyone* can create *many* accounts on the blockchain. The design of the decentralized system will then determine the kind of collusion that can subvert it. If you give each account one vote, then you incentivize the creation of many sock puppet accounts to get extra votes. If you make each vote cost money, then you create a system that again favours the interest of the wealthy over that of the masses, leading to a plutocracy. This is a trade-off that even Butalin admits is going to be hard to solve in an identity-free environment.

In the real world, we already have a centralized answer to the problem. Think about secret ballot elections in a democracy to solve a similar problem. You want to guarantee every citizen a vote, and to protect democracy, you need to ensure no one gets more than one vote. The answer is in the voter ID card issued by the centralized, sovereign government. The voting list in most countries is also a public ledger albeit a centralized one. Everyone is guaranteed a vote, and only one vote. Moreover, the votes are counted, while keeping the voting preferences of each voter secret. If their privacy is not protected, they may be subjected to coercion by those in power.

It is interesting how some simple problems in the centralized world become complex problems in the decentralized world, and vice versa.

Just as we blitzscaled our way into the centralized and monopolized internet, there is a feverish, almost cult-like reverence for decentralization that's gripping the tech world now. If connecting the world was the rallying cry of the centralized web, freedom from regulators/governments seems to be the rallying cry of the decentralized web. There's no doubt in our minds that decentralization offers advantages and protections that the centralized web simply cannot offer. However, the converse is true as well. The decentralized web leaves us vulnerable in ways that the centralized web didn't.

If, heaven forbid, your house gets burned down or flooded and you lose all your documents, you will still be able to go to your bank, prove who you are and get your money. If the bank itself tries to steal your money or goes under, federal insurance on deposits protects citizens from losing all their money. The trust-no-one feature of cryptocurrencies means that if you lose a password, no one can help recover that money. It is estimated that at least 2.56 million coins, i.e., more than US$ 100 billion worth of bitcoins are lost due to forgotten passwords or keys. This isn't just about bitcoins; it happens across all decentralized cryptocurrencies.

The other trade-off is that preventing centralized control means we can't use centralized regulations to prevent things we would not want as a society. Cryptocurrency is disrupting the criminal economy, the way the internet disrupted the regular economy. It is leading to increased sophistication and specialization of the criminal supply chain. As one anonymous researcher said in a ZDnet article. 'The centralization of fraudulent activity in a handful of markets mirrors similar economic and commercial patterns in real-world financial markets. This phenomenon may seem like a ripe opportunity for law enforcement agencies to effectively shut down a sizable portion of cybercriminal activity; however, as we've seen in the past with the shutting down of markets like Alphabay, Hansa, and Silk Road, threat actors quickly migrate their activities to other markets.'

Decentralization is not a silver bullet, and centralization is not always a problem. So how do we design a system that is not under the control of a few players, while also being able to use the law to protect the vulnerable?

To answer this, we need to go back to the other idea that started in 2009, halfway across the world in India.

15

INDIA'S STACKS

IDENTITY CRISIS

The *New Yorker*'s most reproduced cartoon ever is from July 1993. Two dogs are in front of a computer—one sitting atop a swivel chair, with one paw on the keyboard. The dog using the computer is talking to the other dog, seated on the floor, listening intently. 'On the internet, nobody knows you're a dog', reads the caption.

"On the Internet, nobody knows you're a dog."

The cartoon is obviously facetious, but like every great political cartoon, this too managed to put a finger on the heart of the issue in a single panel. Being online was synonymous with being anonymous. The internet connected you with anyone, anywhere in the globe, but no one had any way of knowing who was behind the keyboard.

But this feature of the internet was not very compatible with the business model that eventually powered it. Advertisers needed to know if you are indeed a dog, or a dog parent, or just hate dogs, so that they could sell things to you accordingly. How do they figure this out?

This is the problem of identity. Every individual website or app, for the purposes of analysing traffic, or storing data about you, or transacting with you, or displaying a personalized advertisement, needs to identify if you have visited before. It is a much more involved problem than it appears. Even today, one can't always be entirely certain that on the other end of the line, one is transacting with a human. Although today the offender is more likely to be a bot than a dog.

India in 2009 was also facing a crisis of identity.

A significant portion of its residents lacked formal, individual identity credentials that were universally accepted. Take Rajni, a vegetable seller from rural Maharashtra. Rajni had a voter ID, and was also listed on the family's ration card, though it didn't have her picture on it. But for purposes such as opening a bank account, the voter ID alone is not considered enough, and the ration card identifies a family, not an individual. Rajni was invisible to the system, for no particular fault of hers. When in need, she couldn't borrow at reasonable rates from banks and had to turn to informal money lenders. As an unfortunate consequence, people like Rajni, who needed money the most, had to take the most expensive loans.

On the flip side, the government too could not be sure if all the people on its beneficiary lists were real people who existed or were simply forged entries to siphon resources from the state's welfare budget. The government of India in 2005 estimated that 58 per cent of subsidized foodgrains and 38 per cent of subsidized kerosene disbursed under various government programmes did not reach their intended beneficiaries. Billions of dollars of welfare money from a developing nation were lost to unscrupulous middlemen instead of helping the poor.

On the internet, advertising giants, especially Google and Facebook, set out to solve the identity problem.

Google gave away free email accounts, and Facebook made you create your own profile for free to connect with your friends. This incentivized people to tell them who they were. They invented 'login with Google' and 'login with Facebook', doing away with the need to remember multiple logins and passwords. They even contributed money and effort to open source projects in the space of identity management such as OAuth. These made it possible and convenient to use your Google or Facebook identity on other websites, making it more likely that you would use them as your identity credentials across the web. This also allowed services to integrate better, such that various apps could share your data between themselves. Your social media app, for example, may add birthday reminders to your personal calendar because of a shared identity—your email.

Just as highways, bridges and ports are physical infrastructures, components such as identity or payments are digital infrastructure. They are essential to a smooth internet experience, as roads and railways are to a country's people. Like infrastructure, these systems are complex to build in a safe and secure manner and require specialized talent. They require large investments upfront but also offer economies of scale.

Investing in identity infrastructure on the internet was not just necessary but also lucrative. By building this critical touchpoint that affected every website, ad networks were able to track your activities across the whole web, not just their own products. This allowed them to offer better targeted advertising than anyone else, and led to their dominance in the online advertising market. Advertisers were willing to pay hand over fist for the data these companies had. In 2019, at about US$ 333 billion, the total global spending on digital ads exceeded that of ads in the physical world.

But in India, no private player found it lucrative to solve Rajni's problem.

The US advertising market, online and offline put together, is worth US$ 240 billion. The same number for India is only US$ 8.5

billion, despite having roughly four times as many people. Although Rajni would benefit as much as anyone from the internet and a digital footprint, advertising revenues were just not incentive enough for private players to take Rajni digital.

This is a classic example of what economists call a market failure. India in 2009 realized that to bring the kind of prosperity, progress and convenience that the internet promised, it needed to take digital to everyone, not just the rich.

In the West, private players were willing to invest because of the size of the market, and because they could see people conducting commerce online. In India, even if they could somehow get it to her, people found it hard to imagine what Rajni would do with the internet.

The reality is, tragically, the opposite. In the West, the internet made a lot of new things possible, but it mostly made old things more convenient. To Rajni, the internet brought a world of opportunities she had never experienced before. The internet didn't care if Rajni was illiterate. It could bring her videos of things she'd never seen and help her learn skills she never knew before. She could get welfare benefits digitally, saving her time, money and peace of mind. Rajni could even get a loan, start a business and lift herself out of poverty. The difference that the internet can make to Rajni's life is much more meaningful to her than simply bringing her convenience. Yet, in the advertising model, she gets left behind.

India decided that it was going to have to build its own digital infrastructure. And, crucially, India would build this digital infrastructure as a public good.

PUBLIC GOODS

Economists define public goods as non-rivalrous and non-excludable.

To understand what public goods are, think of the humble street light which, once installed, gives light to everyone equally on the street. Short of destroying the street light, no one can block another person from using it, i.e., street lights are non-excludable. Nor does one person's use of the street light affect the use by another. The same light is shared by all, making street lights non-rivalrous.

We all derive benefit from the street light, but someone has to pay for it. The simple and fair thing to do is that since it benefits all of us, it should be paid for by all of us. This is why governments fund the creation of many public goods with the taxpayer's money. It is not just street lights; public parks, open highways, the public health system, and the public education system are funded with public money. Remember, a public good is not defined by who funds it, but by who can use it. Andrew Carnegie, steel baron from the 1800s and philanthropist, funded the creation of almost 1700 public libraries across the United States. They remain non-excludable and for all practical purposes, non-rivalrous, and so are public goods funded by private capital.

Essential services such as identity, payments and data exchange are critical touchpoints of the internet that all of us need. By allowing these critical touchpoints to be entirely under private control, we give up a lot of power over our digital lives to the companies that build and run this infrastructure.

One simple fallout of letting this infrastructure be private is that they often build it to capture network effects. Network effects are the positive externalities that come from creating a network, because the value of the interconnected whole is more than the sum of its parts. Take the example of WhatsApp versus email. You can send an email from your Gmail account to someone else's Hotmail account. But WhatsApp restricts you from sending messages only to other WhatsApp users. The problem here isn't technical capability, it is a business decision by WhatsApp to capture network effects. Thus, what could be a public good becomes an exclusive club.

In India, the critical digital infrastructure for identity was built by the government instead.

Aadhaar is a digital identity system which has issued a unique identity to more than 1.25 billion residents of India. Residents can authenticate their identity with their own biometrics or by using an OTP, allowing them to prove they are who they claim to be. It is used to solve the problem of identity in many different contexts. But, since Aadhaar is funded by the Indian Government and not designed for targeted advertising, it is designed to collect as little data about you as possible. The logs of authentication, i.e., where you used your

Aadhaar, are designed to protect the privacy of citizens from the UIDAI itself. Moreover, the logs are required by law to be deleted after a certain period.

With the ability to prove their identity at the fingertips of every resident, millions of Indians were no longer invisible to the system.

Between 2011 and 2017, more than half a billion people in India opened a bank account. Simply opening an account may not sound like a big deal. However, for many like Rajni, who had been excluded from the formal financial system, it was their first ever bank account.

These bank accounts then powered the country's move to Direct Benefits Transfer. Corruption in the public welfare delivery system has been a problem hounding India for decades. In 1985, the then prime minister publicly announced that of every rupee spent by the government, only 15 paise reaches the needy. Welfare delivery systems were elaborate. There were many layers and middlemen in the supply chain. Each had discretionary power, and therefore, there was a lot of leakage. With Direct Benefits Transfer, instead of elaborate systems, money could be sent directly into the accounts of those who need it. With a unique identity, the government could also have more confidence in the legitimacy of the beneficiary lists that they maintained.

Of course, Aadhaar is no magic pill. It can't prevent all forms of fraud, nor can it plug every leakage. But it does make it easier, cheaper and faster to prove that you are truly you and make a claim on your benefits while making it harder for fraudsters to forge a claim on the benefits that are yours. It reduces the power that local tyrants and black marketers have over residents, since the subsidy is not going through a middleman.

Aadhaar was the backbone needed to digitize and modernize government welfare delivery experience. A simple example is benefits portability. Earlier, to prevent double-dipping, residents could only purchase ration from the ration shop they were assigned to. With Aadhaar, local governments can track in real-time the subsidy consumed against each account. Since the people's identity was simply a number and their own biometrics, they could authenticate anywhere. So some state governments have done away with the assignment system completely. They allow any citizen to take their ration from any shop, as long as they use Aadhaar to prove *who they are* and not double-dip. This is extremely useful in a country of more than 400 million internal immigrant workers, who travel from their villages to other districts for seasonal employment. The ration shops which used to be mini-monopolies because of the assignment system now faced the heat of competition. Many ration shops started offering home-delivery and other services to attract eligible residents.

There are other advantages to having your own digital public good for identity. In April 2020, the government was able to transfer relief payments to more than 200 million women within a few days because this digital financial infrastructure existed. Aadhaar was also crucial to the rapid rollout of the vaccine program.

However, Digital Public Goods don't always have to look like Aadhaar did. Remember they are public goods because of how they are used, not because of who funds them. One simple example would be Wikipedia. Wikipedia is non-rivalrous and non-excludable. It is not, however, built by a government or any public entity. Wikipedia is run by the not-for-profit Wikimedia Foundation, which in turn gets its money from donations, and also the in-kind efforts of its volunteers and community.

Aadhaar was only the first in a long line of digital infrastructure that India invested in. Once Aadhaar's versatility was understood, India started building layer upon layer of digital infrastructure in other critical areas such as payments and data exchange. The collection of these layers came to be known as the India Stack.

The digital public goods approach has proven itself worthwhile.

As of today, more than US$ 240 billion of subsidies have been transferred directly from the coffers of the government to the intended beneficiaries. This money is leading to an increase in the use of bank accounts. The Bank of International Settlements, the central bank of central banks, in a paper published in 2019, said that the outcomes that India achieved in financial inclusion with digital infrastructure in seven years, would have taken nearly half a century by traditional growth processes.

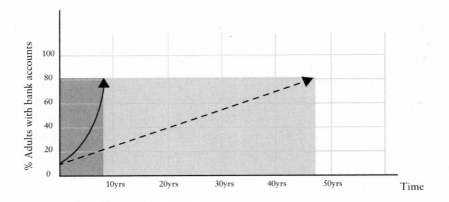

With digital infrastructure, India achieved in 7 years,
what would have taken 47 years.

It was not long before many started wondering if the effect that digital public goods had on financial inclusion, could be repeated in other critical development areas such as improving healthcare access or education outcomes.

WHAT WORKS AT SCALE

What does it take to run a single classroom?

At the bare minimum, you need a set of students at a similar learning level. You need the appropriate content to teach and a teacher familiar with the content to teach it. You'd still need the teachers to be superhuman, as many are, since they would also take on other responsibilities of running the classroom.

In an actual village, children of different ages differ in learning levels, so you need a school, not just a classroom. A school needs multiple teachers, multiple classrooms, and administrators to manage all of it. Learning doesn't end in school. Parents help create a learning environment at home so that children can meet learning outcomes.

When you think about running the entire Indian education system, scale changes everything.

There are more than 1.5 million schools, with nearly 10 million teachers, teaching almost 250 million students in schools. They aren't all learning the same thing, either. There are more than sixty educational boards in thirty-two languages of instruction across the country. Each issues its own curriculum to suit local context, which varies greatly between states.

India's educational system is, to put it mildly, complex and diverse. Technology has the potential to help improve learning outcomes, but the education system is too unwieldy for any single app, portal or platform to manage. It is too complex even for a prescriptive set of features or solutions. The education system isn't one problem to solve. It is just the collective name we give to the 250 million unique learning journeys that we owe to our children and our future.

Often these sorts of grand problems attract grand solutions.

Many in the development sector want to make an impact at scale. They try new ideas in pilots, pick the ones that look most promising and try to scale what works. Many such solutions have seemed promising at the start, but lose their efficacy when scaled up. Some may work at a small scale with a dedicated team, but are too cumbersome to be implemented nationally. Other solutions simply do not work when the context and underlying assumptions are changed as we scale up from one region to multiple others.

In the face of this complexity and diversity, we need a humbler approach. Instead of governments or even not-for-profits trying to 'solve' the problem at a large scale, we need to distribute the ability for people to solve their own problems. Instead of scaling what works, we need to ask:

What works at scale?

Energized textbooks are a great example of something that works at scale. Energized textbooks distribute the ability to solve, rather than solve a problem. Students often have trouble understanding the concepts from their primary material. Energized textbooks have mapped individual learning concepts to QR codes that are pre-printed in textbooks. Any capable device can scan the code to identify the concept and retrieve additional digital content to help learning. The magical part is that the content can be much more suited to the child's actual needs—eg. explanation videos, practice questions, interactive simulations and worksheets—delivered in the local language.

Take Rui. Rui is a smart, energetic and lively five-year-old and studies in a government primary school. Her school-educated mother is worried that Rui is not ready for grade 1—she cannot read well or write in Marathi; they speak Urdu at home. Rui's mother consults Rui's teacher, who shows her the QR codes of the concepts Rui struggles with.

Rui's father used the codes to print worksheets, download videos and activities on his phone. Rui and her mother now listen to stories, learn new words and do math activities using utensils, sticks, and stones available in and around the house. After her dad gets home, Rui loves beating her own high score in a game of identifying letters, words and number operations. Her dad got the link to the game from one of the QR codes in her textbook.

Energized textbooks allowed more than thirty-five state and central boards of India to roll out digital content for school education in over thirty languages. More than 600 million printed textbooks with 10 billion QR codes are now being used by school children and teachers all around the country.

Energized textbooks are one example of a 'building block'.

By itself, each building block performs a simple, atomic function. The energized textbook by itself, is just a regular textbook, with some QR codes printed in it. But when you combine that with other building blocks, you start to get solutions that can really impact learning outcomes.

India has built DIKSHA, a digital infrastructure for education, consisting of many such building blocks. It is designed to deal with the complexity and diversity of India by not being overly prescriptive. Even the assumption of always-on connectivity cannot be taken for granted. Teachers as well as students use DIKSHA to learn and to share what they've learnt. DIKSHA works at scale. More than 3.6 billion learning sessions have taken place on DIKSHA, accounting for a total of more than forty-four billion minutes.

DIKSHA, in turn, is based on the open-source Sunbird digital public good, developed and maintained by EkStep Foundation. Sunbird was a counterintuitive solution to the problem of education. Instead of aiming to serve a finished dish, Sunbird aims to give everyone the ingredients they need via building blocks.

The building blocks in Sunbird have been proven to be useful in more than just school education. Sunbird's credentialing mechanism, which allows students to record their school achievements, was quickly adapted to create DIVOC—Digital Infrastructure for Vaccination Open Credentialing. Basically, as we all got COVID-19 vaccines, we needed a safe, reliable, cheap and privacy-protecting way of proving that we were vaccinated. Left to themselves, each vaccination centre would have issued a certificate in their own format. As the world reopened, it would be hard to confirm if someone was holding a genuine certificate. DIVOC provided a digital standard that all vaccination centres could adhere to, which couldn't be spoofed easily, and could be verified by anyone. Each one of the more than a billion doses of vaccines given in India via COWIN comes with a DIVOC-enabled vaccination certificate.

Instead of the 'scale what works' approach, which first determines a solution and then tries to impose it at scale, the 'what works at scale' approach only determines what blocks to create. Solutions emerge from the creativity and gumption of the people. The best part is the surprising ways in which people reuse and remix these blocks into surprisingly creative solutions.

A building block approach to digital public goods is being followed in healthcare as well. The Ayushman Bharat Digital Mission (ABDM) aims to develop the backbone necessary to support the integrated digital health infrastructure of the country. It creates the missing links between the various health providers in our country, and allows patients to see a unified view of their health data. The Health Stack, as it is called, is starting from scratch, including creating its own health ID. By starting with a new health ID, the ABDM allows users much more granular control over their identity, their data and its privacy.

There is still an important role for the private sector in a Digital Public Goods future. While infrastructure is essential and must be built, much of the delight on the internet comes from private innovation and start-ups trying new ideas. We can't throw out the baby with the bathwater. For a successful Digital Public Good, we also need to think about how we can create the right incentives for private players to continue to innovate and deliver better, faster and cheaper services that are aligned with user needs.

This was the intent behind India's other big digital public good success story, the Unified Payments Interface, or UPI. If we want a vibrant future, both the public and private sectors need to be building technology as per their vision. The question isn't either public or private.

The real question is how do we work better *together*?

16

ARCHITECTING THE FUTURE

PROTOCOLS AND INTEROPERABILITY

The art of bitfulness shows how to mindfully use technology for our personal use. However, that's only going to treat the symptoms, not the cause.

As we said in Part One, our relationship with technology is a two-way street. We don't usually stop to ask why a certain software is architected a certain way. We don't think about what constraints drove its design, and what that design does to us. However, just because we don't pay attention to something, doesn't mean it isn't capable of influencing us.

If we want to fix The Third Crisis, we need to become more mindful of our relationship as a society with our collective technology.

There probably is no better example of fixing our relationship with our collective technology than digital payments in India. For a country of more than 1.3 billion, there are only 30 million credit cards in India. Cash is still dominant here. In 2016, the Indian government demonetized select currency notes and nudged the economy towards formal, digital modes of payments.

However, unlike the west, credit cards were not going to be enough. India needed a low-cost, fast payment technology that could work on mobile phones, when on the go. There are many private players operating in the mobile payments space globally. Most take their inspiration from the success of mobile payments in China where two giants, Alibaba and WeChat, have split the market between them. Alibaba, WeChat and their global copycats crafted their 'wallets' as closed-loop systems— users could only pay other users of the same wallet. The closed-loop design is not a necessity of mobile payments technology. It is a deliberate exclusionary design to capture network effects.

This is why, in 2016, the National Payments Corporation of India (NPCI) launched the interoperable Unified Payments Interface, more popularly known as UPI. In the five years hence, the success of UPI has been tremendous. As of October 2021, there were more than 4.2 billion transactions taking place monthly on UPI, transacting a value of over INR 7.71 lakh crores (about US$103 billion). UPI now makes up 10 per cent of all retail payments, and the total value transacted annually comes to about 30 per cent of the country's GDP. In just eighteen months since launch, the volume of transactions on the network exceeded the combined volumes of credit-card and debit- card transactions in India. UPI has allowed the Indian economy to sustain cashless, contactless transactions when it most needed it. First, in 2016–17, when cash supply was low as select currency notes were demonetized. Also, in 2020–21 when due to the pandemic, transactions had to be done remotely and with minimal contact.

However, UPI is not a platform, it is a protocol.

Transactions via UPI (Digital Fast payments)

Source: ACI Worldwide Real-Time payments report

A protocol is simply a set of rules that makes coordination simpler.

The simplest example of a protocol is the set of basic traffic rules in a country. Everyone agrees to drive on the left (or right) side of the road to avoid collisions. There is nothing special about either direction: the benefit comes from everyone being coordinated.

Protocols establish a shared language of communication between all participants of the network. Irrespective of their own internal processes, structure or design, all participants can coordinate through shared protocols. The internet is itself a suite of protocols implemented across billions of devices that direct traffic of data packets. Which is why, the IP in IP address stands for Internet Protocol. All the devices on the internet are, thus, speaking the same language and can understand each other.

UPI defined a standard set of rules around the sending and receiving of money in the Indian banking system. It allowed any two banks, which may be running their own custom software in the backend, to be able to talk to each other in a shared language. Moreover, since this shared language is a public good, it was available to private players to build innovative apps and services on top of it. It made payments interoperable, and unbundled the payments transaction interface from the bank account provider.

In simpler words, you could now use a State Bank of India app to transfer money from your Citibank account to a friend using the Google Pay app to manage their HDFC bank account. You could even consolidate bank accounts from multiple banks under one app. All users can register a payment address, such as nikhil.kumar@upi. Anyone using any payment app can send money to that address without knowing the underlying bank details or even which bank they transact with.

UPI opened up competition and innovation in the digital payments sector without encouraging a walled garden or a monopoly. UPI users can easily change providers if they believe that their current provider is not meeting their expected level of service or is violating their privacy. Because each transaction is linked to a Know Your Customer verified bank account, there is no added risk of misuse.

Protocols can work without central platforms, and thus, already offer protection against monopoly. All modern email works on the Send Mail Transfer Protocol (SMTP). The wonderful thing about

SMTP is that it has been designed to be interoperable. Each of us can have our own email address provider, and use different email apps on our phones and desktops. Unlike instant messaging, which requires the sender and receiver to be on the same app, you can send an email to anyone with a valid email address. You are not tied to any particular platform. New start-ups can create better email clients. Existing users will not need to give up their existing email IDs, or forgo old emails. Thus, interoperable protocols reduce the costs of switching between services and make competition possible.

Protocols are not a radical new invention. They are how the original architects of the internet built it. The internet started as a tool for academic and military knowledge sharing, built from research and defence spending. The early architects were remarkably self-aware of what they were building—a shared infrastructure. Hence, they had a deep commitment to interoperability. The driving concern was not to 'escape competition'. This reflected in the architecture of the open networks they had built. Somewhere since the original sin, we've faltered.

Even before digital, we have required interoperability from our other network infrastructure. Telecom services do not require both users to be on the same network, you can call any number irrespective of who their provider is. Telecom companies are also required to provide mobile number portability. That is, TelCos must provide a mechanism to change providers without the user facing the inconvenience of changing their phone number. We should be demanding the same from modern digital infrastructure.

Protocol-driven interoperability is probably our most effective tool against concentration. Remember, there is nothing technically stopping these platforms from being open: it is a careful business decision to not do so. Instead of regulating their behaviour, which is often hard, countries can think of a combination of a digital public good such as a protocol, and a law which compels internet platforms to be interoperable to the protocol.

There is now an effort to apply these principles to the markets where aggregators operate. Beckn is a not-for-profit organization building an open protocol for distributed commerce. Beckn aims to create interoperable networks of sellers, starting with the domain of ride-sharing and final-mile delivery. It creates a shared infrastructure whereby each of the sellers can come to the network directly, through their preferred service provider. However, once on the network, these sellers are interoperable. This means that a cab on the Beckn network is available through any ride-sharing app on the Beckn network. This means drivers and users have portability, the way our mobile numbers are portable.

Protocols do not kill platforms, they simply change what they do and how they compete. Protocols make platforms amenable to competitive pressures. In the blitzscaling models, competitors would have to reinvent the wheel. They would have to make their own competing network, and spend on acquiring users to make the network viable. Via interoperability, protocols make it easy for anyone to build alternatives to part or whole of the dominant platforms.

Interoperability dramatically reduces the cost of switching services. Your data is not lost to a walled garden when you leave. Individual sellers are independent and have a choice between the platforms that are aggregating demand. The aggregator platforms will not cease to exist. However, the strategic playing field changes considerably.

Without lock-ins to protect their network, a blitzscaling strategy only makes it easier for the next competitor to poach your customers once you've spent money on acquiring them. The network effects accrue at the network level, rather than with any one player. Users can select providers that suit their own privacy levels and feature requirements. This forces innovation and competition to focus on what users want rather than use large amounts of capital to buy the loyalty of users and suffocate competitors.

Today, the private provision of digital infrastructure has led us to outcomes where even what truly belongs to us is being captured by internet startups.

For example, the data around traffic and congestion in a city. Uber and Google Maps have better information about things like how transportation is affected by weather patterns. This data could help us understand and build better physical infrastructure to decongest cities. However, scientists do not often get access to this data, and even when they do, it is costly or comes with strings attached. Even though this data is generated by the public, it is not a public good.

Interoperable protocols solve many problems with the current blitzscaling approach, but not all of them. Private platforms will continue to provide major services due to the size of their investments, the speed of their execution and their innovation. However, their current business model requires controlling access over the generated data.

We must remember that even if it is their network, it is still *our* data.

THEIR NETWORKS, OUR DATA

The COVID-19 pandemic disrupted all our lives.

Social distancing and the lockdown disrupted all our routines, but for some, the shock went much further than that. For many individuals and small businesses, the accelerated move towards digital led to adverse financial impact. Incomes dried up, and expenses, especially medical ones, threatened to destabilize families. Even businesses that were doing well needed capital to make it through the tough times.

Our financial system was not prepared for this system-wide demand for credit. The process to obtain a loan requires time, patience and paperwork—all three of which were harder to come by during the pandemic. This often led to individuals and small businesses turning to the informal sector for capital. The informal money lending market is usurious. It places unfair terms on the borrower, and the collection process can be very unpleasant. However, people flock to it because it is able to deliver credit to the needy with a speed that the formal sector is still unable to match.

Ultimately, it takes money to make money. Without access to credit, the poor are sentenced to poverty forever.

India has under-penetration of formal credit. Indian households aren't borrowing from banks as much as households in other countries. A few bad apples amongst the borrowers have made banks hesitant. Banks do not lend to those without collateral to back a loan. Hence, the poor in this country never get that first seed capital to improve their lives.

Financial data can sort the good apples from the bad. It provides insights into your spending habits, your discipline, etc. However, this data is in different silos in different accounts with various providers.

Today, your financial services providers keep your data locked with themselves for compliance and safety and do not share it with anyone. This practice may be safe, but the tragedy is that if we could liberate this data, it could change millions of lives.

India's Account Aggregator network allows this data to be read together in a secure and encrypted manner.

On 2 September 2021, eight banks joined the Account Aggregator network. Three hundred million bank accounts now can share their data seamlessly, securely and instantly with any financial service provider that requests it.

The Account Aggregators themselves will not be able to read your data. They are consent managers. Think of them as traffic cops that direct data from one place to another. They are simply collecting your consent to share your data from one account to another. They also enforce the conditions under which this sharing must occur.

Account Aggregators act as fiduciaries to you. That is, just like a personal financial advisor, AAs are legally obliged to act in your best interest and can't have a conflict of interest. When a technology like AA empowers people with their data, they can take charge of their financial lives. Their data fills a gap that the collateral offered: to demonstrate trustworthiness.

When the masses can establish trust based on their data, it offers banks a chance to extend a loan even when there is no underlying asset to back up the loan. Moreover, since the data comes directly from the source financial institution, there is no physical paperwork to check. There is also no collateral to inspect. Aadhaar and the India Stack had already solved the problem of identity verification. This means someone can apply for a loan, get approved and receive it in their bank account, all digitally—faster than you get groceries delivered.

This is not a tall claim. Already, the Open Credit Enablement Network (OCEN) rails have been used in closed beta by sole proprietors on the government's e-marketplace (GEM) procurement platform under a program called SAHAY. These sellers are typically small vendors who suffer from a lack of access to credit. Loans ranging from Rs 238 to loans worth Rs 3,98,600 were disbursed, all under ten minutes and digitally to qualifying suppliers. In the feedback video made after the loans were disbursed one supplier called the loan '*doobte ka sahara*' (a lifesaver), whereas others simply called it a 'miracle'.

The Account Aggregator network is part of India's ambitious Data Empowerment and Protection Architecture (DEPA). Our usual conversations around data have always focused on privacy and protection. What is missing from these conversations is the power of self-determination that control over your own data brings. Remember, privacy is boundary management. Sometimes, even with the best intentions, the boundaries others set may not be in our own best interests. DEPA and AA believe that the user is best placed to determine their own boundaries, in a way that best enables them to live their own lives. We need to build protections, but we must empower, not mollycoddle, the user.

DEPA's principles can be expanded to data in any sector, not just financial services. We can imagine a future where our social media, ridesharing, e-commerce and other such data too is being aggregated by consent managers.

The first and second wave of internet companies traded free services for capturing our identity and our data. We were not paying for it, so we became the product. It is hard to judge this trade-off in black-and-white terms. What we can say is this:

Trading control over our data and our digital infrastructure in exchange for services may have been how the internet was *built*. But it cannot be how it *sustains*.

The future is not inevitable, it is a blank page. We need to decide as a collective what we're going to write on it.

SUSTAINING THE FUTURE

Whether it is software or buildings, architects do not get enough credit.

Through the seemingly innocuous placement of doors, windows and walls, architects make decisions like how much sunlight we get and the acoustics of a space. Using the same elements, they make palaces grand or prisons bleak. They make libraries quiet and music halls loud, or frustrate us by doing the opposite.

The architectural considerations of the buildings we work and live in usually recede into the background. But they are ever-present, influencing our behaviours in subtle and sometimes profound ways.

The same goes for software.

We need to become much more aware of how our digital infrastructure is architected, and how this architecture is affecting all of us. If we continue building our digital infrastructure the way we do, we risk concentration of power in every industry. To get out of this Third Crisis, there are no easy answers and no clear villains.

But, we stand in a unique moment in history. The digitization of our lives presents our generation with an opportunity to rethink and rebuild the fundamental architecture of our society. Instead of mindlessly going along for the ride, our most meaningful choice is to stop, pause and really think about the future we would like to build.

Can we build a future where the leading technology is one that serves us better rather than technology that is better at making us serve it?

If we think of our collective technology as a public good and not an opportunity for blitzscaling, we can. The good news is that building digital public goods is neither very hard, nor very expensive, if we are smart about its design. As with UPI, the actual digital public good may be as simple as designing a protocol. The early drafts of the protocol were written by a team of three technologists put together by NPCI, in their spare time. There are not-for-profit think tanks, such as iSPIRT, which contribute volunteer expertise and time towards the task of building and promoting digital infrastructure such as the India Stack and now the Health Stack. Seeking a different challenge, and looking to make an impact with their work, high-quality tech talent with previous experience in global tech firms now work at not-for-profits such as Beckn or EkStep to create digital public goods and building blocks. One notable example is Dr. Pramod Varma. In 2009, he was Chief Technology Architect at the global technology company, Sterling Commerce, a part of IBM. He quit his job to design digital public goods for India. He was Chief Architect of Aadhaar and played a key role in the architecture of Beckn, DEPA, EkStep, and UPI, amongst others. The actual work of writing code, hosting it on servers and maintaining it still costs money, and depending on the task, can be funded by private players, philanthropists or even the government.

The funding of these digital public goods can also be supported by a digital tax.

Already European countries are demanding a digital tax, because online firms often take advantage of tax residency in a country with low tax rates, while operating globally. The revenues from the digital tax can be directed towards creating digital public good alternatives to critical infrastructure where there is threat of concentration.

The digital tax can be waived or reduced for those companies that are interoperable with the underlying digital public good. This way, when private infrastructure usage or walled gardens start to go up, so does the digital tax collected. The tax collected can be used for funding competing digital public goods. As the industry moves towards more open infrastructure and interoperability, the tax collected from these industries automatically reduces. These self-regulating mechanisms create both the incentive to be interoperable, as well as the funds to create an interoperable alternative if companies choose not to be.

Digital Public Goods, thus, offer a public-policy solution that is much more effective than regulations for a simple reason: it is proactive rather than reactive.

Regulations try to coerce companies into following both the letter and spirit of the law, through the use of penalties, punishments and permissions. However, in Digital Public Goods, the code is the law. User rights can be enshrined in the architecture of the underlying design itself. Privacy and anti-trust rules can be embedded into the design. For example, no private operator on UPI can block payments to a specific competitor. If they do, they risk losing their access to the network. Of course, we will still need supporting laws and policies, but they have a much better chance of being implemented well if there's an underlying DPG.

Digital Public Goods also make our collective data generated by the underlying digital infrastructure into a public good. The anonymized insights from our behaviour as a collective will be available to citizens, scientists and entrepreneurs alike. We can channel this data into research and development, better governance, or to make services like insurance cheaper.

A lot of these goals are shared by the decentralized web. A public blockchain is non-rivalrous and non-excludable by definition, and thus, a public good. We do not believe that there is even a debate between centralized versus decentralized technologies. They are both different philosophies of building technologies, and each offers different trade-offs of advantages and disadvantages.

While a centralized system and its creators have tremendous power, they can be held accountable with the force of law. A decentralized system has no leader issuing orders, and instead depends on the infallibility of its code and economic incentive structure to keep the system running as intended. Neither one is 'better'. In fact, the best probable outcome for us as a society is two thriving ecosystems. This gives users the choice between these two different systems. The force of competition between them will nudge both to keep innovating and improving.

If you believe that the reason for our current set of problems is because some corporation is evil, you'd be wrong. The concept of good and evil is not sufficient to describe the complex set of incentives and interactions that drive the behaviour of platforms and people. Like we described with the SaySafe example in Chapter 13, even with good intentions, companies can end up on the Slippery Slopes of Scale.

Ultimately, this book is not anti-tech, it is pro-you.

Our essential argument here is that the digital infrastructure we create has significant influence over our lives, and thus, is too important to be left *only* to the private sector to control. The current model, *blitzscaling*, prizes the full and complete capture of user time, attention and data above all else. They fund building the underlying infrastructure as a winner-take-all to support this goal and 'escape competition'. The private sector brings innovation and choice to the table, while the public sector brings stability and inclusion.

The real trick is achieving *balance*.

Governments, civil society and the private sector each play an important part in our society. They each have their own strengths, weaknesses and blind spots. Letting any one of them have absolute control over our technology is probably not a good idea. We need to find a way to build Societal Platforms. That is, where everyone in society plays their respective part in shaping our collective technology, and hence, shaping our collective future.

Our proposal for the future is not very radical. In 2005, Stanford held a big event to commemorate the birth of the internet. They revealed a plaque acknowledging not one creator, but about thirty people working in different teams at different universities. The plaque acknowledges that even that list of thirty is incomplete. It says, 'Ultimately, thousands if not tens to hundreds of thousands have contributed their expertise to the evolution of the internet'.

This is a heartening representation of what the internet was supposed to be. The internet was supposed to be a way for curious humans to share knowledge with each other, even if they are oceans apart. The point was that ideas are non-rivalrous. As George Bernard Shaw had said, 'if you have an idea and I have an idea and we exchange these ideas, then each of us will have two ideas.'

The internet, our social networks, and our marketplaces are too important to be controlled by anyone. They should belong, simultaneously, to all of us, and to none of us.

Now is the time we architect that future.

APPENDIX

The Art of Bitfulness is about having a mindful relationship with your technology. We do this by managing our time, attention and privacy thoughtfully. Given below is a set of tools that could help you on this journey. Chapters 5—12 provide detailed instructions on how to integrate these tools into your life. This appendix is also available online at bitfulness.com/links, or you can scan the QR code below.

MANAGING TIME

The single biggest problem with our smartphones is how much time we lose to them. The tools below can help change the way we use our devices. Chapters 5 (How to Think Clearly) and 6 (What to Think About) provide more detail on how to spend our time on our devices better.

1.   Use a note-taking software for thinking

- Evernote (Windows, Mac, Android, iOS, browser extension)
- Roam Research (Windows, Mac, Linux)
- Obsidian (Windows, Mac, Android, iOS, Linux)
- Notion (Windows, Mac, Android, iOS)
- Google Keep (Android, iOS, Chrome, browser extension)
- OneNote (iOS, Windows, Mac, Android, Windows Phone, Apple Watch, browser extension)
- Simplenote (iOS, Android, Windows, Mac, Linux, Linux, browser extension)

2.   Use Bitfulness Meditation to take charge of the moment

The amount of information available to us can often overwhelm us. As we try to focus and make good use of our time, the first step is to be able to calm the mind. We recommend journaling in your note-taking software to declutter your mind. Detailed instructions about this exercise and how to process your thoughts are available in Chapter 5.

3.   Time blocking

Reduce friction in your workflow by designating specific blocks of time for different activities. This helps maintain context and eliminate interruptions. Always block time for your most important tasks first. Treat this time as non-negotiable.

Fill in the remaining time with other tasks, like meetings. You can allot blocks of time for distracting tasks such as checking email or surfing the web. Having done that, try not to do these tasks outside of this time block. Here are some calendar apps that help you time-block quickly and easily.

- Google Calendar
- Clockify
- Skedpal
- Plan
- Hourstack

- TogglTrack
- Calendly

4. Create a Time Budget

Even though time is more valuable than money, people pinch pennies but waste hours. Create a time budget so that you have access to high-level awareness of where your time *should* be going. A detailed description is given in Chapter 6 (What to Think About), under the heading Using Time. This table is available digitally on bitfulness. com/time.

MANAGING ATTENTION

Technological conveniences come with massive flows of information. Get free from information overload by being smart about where your attention goes. Since you have finite mindspace, occupy it with tasks that matter to you. Given below are some tools for dividing your attention in a savvy way.

Split Your Personality

The noisier your environment, the less likely you are to focus. Using new user accounts allows you to create different virtual environments for different kinds of focus. Chapters 7-10 describe in detail how to create three personalities to get into three modes of attention.

1. Create a new User Account

It is easier to make a new user account sparse and clean than to make your current user account less distracting. Here are the steps to create a new user on your device.

- **On an Android phone:** Go to Settings (gear icon) → Users/Users and Accounts → Click the add user button → Sign in to your Google account (you can use a different email for this user profile if you want) → Calls and SMSes are disabled by default—you can change that if you like.

- To change, switch back to your main user account. To switch accounts, pull the notification shade down and tap the user icon. You'll see a list of users. Select your main account → Go to Settings → Users → Select the user you just created → Tap the gear icon → Switch on turn on phone calls and SMS.
- **On an Apple computer:** Go to System Preferences → Users and Groups → If the lock at the bottom left is locked, click to unlock and change your settings → Click the plus sign to add a user → Choose type of user (admin/standard/sharing-only) → Enter a name and password and click 'Create'.
- **On a Windows XP, 2000, 2003, Vista or Windows 7 PC:** Start → Control Panel → User Accounts and Family Safety → Add or Remove User Accounts → Create New Account → Choose between Standard, Admin, and Guest → Log out and log in to toggle between users.
- **On a Windows 10 PC:** Go to Settings → Accounts → Family and Other People → Add someone else to this PC → In the Microsoft Account window that pops up, click 'I don't have this person's sign-in information' → On the next page, click 'Add a user without a Microsoft account' → Type in the login details for your new user, and click 'Next' → You're redirected to the list of users within Settings.
- **On iOS devices** (iPad and iPhone): iOS does not allow for multiple users for legal accountability, traceability and security reasons. However, you could use different email services for each profile. For example, Outlook for work, Gmail for personal communication, iOS Mail app for creative work.

2. Use a website blocker

Web browsers are rife with distractions that encourage mindless scrolling. Block these distractions during specific periods of time, or even permanently. Here is a list of browser-based website blockers.

- StayFocusd (Chrome)
- LeechBlock (Chrome, Firefox, Opera, Brave, Vivaldi, Edge) – Browser extension

- Limit (Chrome)
- WasteNoTime (Safari, Chrome)
- Pause (Chrome)

3.   Batch your notifications

To remain mindful about notifications, turn off the non-essential ones. You can also toggle your notification settings so that certain notifications are silent. However, you might end up checking your phone more often to see whether you have missed anything important. One solution is to have your notifications sent to you at specific intervals of time. Here's how to do that.

- **iPhones** have an in-built option to schedule notifications. To do this, go to Settings → Notifications → Schedule Summary. Now, select the apps whose notifications you would like to batch → Choose the times at which you would like to receive notification summaries. The default is twice a day; you can tap 'Add Summary' if you'd like more than one.
- If you have an **Android** device, here are some apps that you can use to manage your notifications:

    - Batch
    - Daywise
    - Spren

4.   Use the in-built focus mode

If your work cannot allow for batching notifications, filter non-essential notifications using your phone's in-built focus mode. Customize this mode to allow specific notifications and block others.

- **For iPhone users:** Go to Settings → Focus.
- Apple offers five default focus profiles to choose from: Do not Disturb, Driving, Personal, Sleep, and Work. You can click on each one and take a look at the in-built notification settings. If you're happy with the default profiles, use them.

- If not, you can select the + icon on the Focus page to add a new mode. Customize this profile as you wish. You can even automate or schedule when it switches on. For example, you could choose to schedule Sleep mode at 11 pm every night.
- **For Android users:** Go to Settings → Digital Wellbeing. Here [bitfulness.com/focusandroid] is how to use it.

5. Block access to distracting apps

Eliminate disruptive influences by restricting access to apps where you tend to waste time. Here are some apps that help you regulate what you have access to and how much time you spend there.

- Freedom (Windows, Mac, iOS and Android)
- Forest for gamified focus (iOS, Android)
- Cold Turkey Blocker (Windows, Mac)
- SelfControl (Mac)

6. Streamline your Home Screen

Remove distracting apps from your home screen to help yourself get to the work that really matters. Here are some launchers for **Android** phones that are meant to increase productivity and make it easier for you to focus.

- Minimalist Productivity Launcher for Focus & Goals
- Ratio
- Niagara
- Lawnchair
- Indistractable
- Olauncher

7. Merge your inboxes

The content from all your inboxes—messages, emails, SMSes—can get overwhelming and lead to a lot of tedious scrolling. One simple solution is to get an all-in-one inbox that merges all your textual communication. Here are a few. Don't forget to use the archive and delete options liberally.

- Franz (Windows, Mac, Linux)
- Rambox (Mac)
- All-In-One Messenger (Windows, Mac, Linux)
- IM+ (Mac, iOS, Android)
- Disa (Android)

MANAGING PRIVACY

Our current relationship with technology means that we cannot give up our devices in order to remain 'off the grid'. We can, nonetheless, be smart about how we use technology. Resist getting overwhelmed and paranoid; instead, take these few simple steps to stay protected. Here are some simple steps that will cover against the most common privacy threats and identity theft.

1. Use Password Managers

Reusing the same password or variations of it is how most security breaches happen. Your passwords should be long, rememberable to you, but unguessable. Skip the hassle of trying to memorize multiple secure passwords by using a password manager. These have in-built password generators that churn out complex passwords. Here are some password manager apps you can use.

- LastPass (Windows, Mac, Linux, Chrome, Safari, Firefox, Opera, Edge)
- Keeper (Windows, Mac, Linux, Android, Chrome, Safari, Firefox, Opera, Edge)
- Avira (Windows, Mac, iOS, Android)
- DashLane (Chrome)
- Bitwarden (Windows, Mac, Linux, iOS, Android, Chrome, Firefox, Safari, Edge)

2.   Use a temporary email address

Email addresses are one of the most requested pieces of information online. You might be filling a form or surfing websites that force you to sign up to gain access to their content. Sharing your actual email address might lead to a flood of unwanted promotional emails. Here's where temporary email addresses come in useful. Since they expire within a set period of time, they make for secure anonymous correspondence and file transfers as well. Here are some websites that provide temporary email service:

- https://tempmail.dev/
- https://10minutemail.com/
- https://www.guerrillamail.com/
- https://www.throwawaymail.com/en
- https://temporarymail.com/

3.   Virtual Number

Keep your personal phone number private by using a virtual number. It's common to have to verify an account login or signup by using your phone number. Giving out your actual phone number might lead to spam or make you vulnerable to security leaks.

- Doosra
- Receive SMSes—to receive one-time SMSes

4.   Get end-to-end encrypted email

Using an encrypted email service protects you against snooping. Here are some secure email services with whom you can create an account.

- ProtonMail (Also has Android, iOS apps)
- Tutanota (Also has Android, iOS, Linux, Windows, Mac apps)
- Mailfence
- Hushmail
- Mailbox

5. List of open DNSes

DNSes translate readable addresses like 'www.google.com' into a format that computers can process. The translated address is public, making it possible for third parties to log your web activity. Change your DNS into a safe public DNS, the top several of which are listed below:

- Google: 8.8.8.8
- Quad9: 9.9.9.9
- OpenDNS Home: 208.67.222.222
- Cloudflare: 1.1.1.1
- CleanBrowsing: 185.228.168.9
- Alternate DNS: 76.76.19.19
- AdGuard DNS: 94.140.14.14

Go to bitfulness.com/changedns for a step-by-step on how to change your DNS server on your router.

6. Anti-Malwares

Malwares are all kinds of malicious software, including viruses. Malware attacks often hold your computer hostage and steal your passwords and usernames. Anti-malwares protect your device from phishing, ransomware and key-logging. See below for some well-known anti-malwares.

- Malware Bytes
- Avast
- Comodo
- AVG
- Spybot

7. General dos and don'ts

- Don't use public Wi-Fi
- Log out of public computers every time you use them
- Never re-use your passwords

- Be careful of what you post on social media
- Check your privacy settings from time to time

8. Extra protection measures

- Use a VPN
- Use a secure browser, like Tor
- Pay anonymously and securely (cash, cryptocurrency)
- Delete your search history and Google activity regularly
- Switch to a secure messaging platform like Signal or Jitsi.

ACKNOWLEDGEMENTS

The book cover says this book is by Nandan Nilekani and Tanuj Bhojwani. However, we consider that to be an oversimplification. This book is built on inputs and ideas from many people, and we are grateful to each and every one of them.

First of all, we'd like to thank Arun Mohan Sukumar, Matt Sheehan, NS Ramnath, Onaiza Drabu, Rahul Matthan, Ramachandra Guha, Rob Fitzpatrick and Samar Halarnkar, who offered words of encouragement and advice, drawing from their own experience of writing books. If you like our words, you'll love theirs.

Brave souls like Kamya Chandra, Karthik Sivaram, Mandakini Chandra and Priyanka Asera volunteered to be our test readers and suffered through the early drafts so that you didn't have to. We are very grateful to them.

Secondly, we'd like to thank the teams from iSpirt and EkStep for their extraordinary patience. The volunteers and builders at these organizations make the work you read about (in Part Three of the book) a reality. We'd like to thank Karthik KS, Pramod Varma, Sanjay Jain, Shankar Maruwada, Sharad Sharma, Siddharth Shetty, Sudhanshu Shekhar and Vivek Raghavan for their support. A special mention to Sanjay Purohit of Societal Platforms and Viraj Tyagi of eGov Foundation for always being available to answer our questions.

What we wrote wouldn't be so slick without our in-house and Penguin India's design and editorial teams. Special thanks to

Meru Gokhale, who called the first draft of this manuscript incoherent (and rightly so). Along the way, we had editorial guidance from Sandra Wendel, and a herculean effort from Ila Deep to get every detail correct. We'd also like to thank Akangksha Sharma, Aparna Abhijit, and Shreya Punj from Penguin for helping put polish on the book and its cover. Most of the diagrams you see in the text are from Esha Singh and Nancy, who have been very patient with our frequently changing requests.

It is not just what goes into the book, though. The most valuable contribution came from those who have kept us calm and sane during the hardest parts of the writing process, in an already hard pandemic year. Tanuj would like to thank his friends Anna Rego, Deepender Singla, Hobbes, Meghana Reddyreddy, Mubeen Masudi, Naman Pugalia, Nikhil Kumar, Prabhkiran Singh, Prajakta Kuwalekar, Roshni Durai Rajan, Sahil Kini, Sambhunath Barik, Shalini Prasad, Srijoni Sen, Susan Atai, and Vivek Nair for being available when he needed them. There is a big list of people who have helped us in many little ways. We remain thankful to all of them.

Both authors are grateful to their family for putting up with their obsession to retreat and write. We can only hope they find this book worth the sacrifices they made for us.

Finally, thank you, dear reader. We've been told reliably by many in the publishing industry that no one reads acknowledgements anymore. So, if you're reading this sentence, know that we're grateful to you for getting this far. We hope it was worth your time. Find a little treat for yourself at https://bitfulness.com/thankyou.